Spanish
phrase book

How To Use This Book

We suggest that you start with the Pronunciation section (pp. 6–9), then turn to Basic Expressions (pp. 10–19). These sections give you some useful words, phrases, and short dialogs and help you get used to pronouncing and using the language.

Consult the Contents pages (pp. 2–5) for the section you need. In each chapter you'll find travel facts, hints, and useful information. Sample phrases are followed by translations and pronunciation.

Look for special YOU MAY HEAR and YOU MAY SEE boxes that highlight phrases that someone may say to you or signs you may see during your travels.

Read along with the dialog boxes (e.g. IN A CAFÉ) that present short, useful conversations. An audio recording of the dialogs in this book can be heard in the Cassette Pack and CD Pack versions.

If you want to know the meaning of a word, your fastest look-up is via the Dictionary section (pp. 168–214).

If you wish to learn about constructing sentences, check the Grammar in the Reference section (pp. 215–223).

Note the color margins are indexed to help you quickly locate the section you need.

If you have difficulty speaking and understanding the language, you can hand the phrase book to the Spanish speaker; each of you can then point to the appropriate phrase or sentence.

Layout: Media Content Marketing, Inc.

CONTACTING THE EDITORS
Every effort has been made to provide accurate information in this publication, but changes are inevitable. The publisher cannot be responsible for any resulting loss, inconvenience or injury. We would appreciate it if readers would call our attention to any errors or outdated information by contacting Berlitz Publishing, PO Box 7910, London SE1 1WE, England. Fax: (44) 20 7403 0290.   email: berlitz@apaguide.demon.co.uk

TABLE OF CONTENTS

PRONUNCIATION

This section is designed to make you familiar with the sounds of Spanish using our simplified phonetic transcription. You'll find the pronunciation of the Spanish letters and sounds explained below, together with their "imitated" equivalents. This system is used throughout the phrase book: simply read the pronunciation as if it were English, noting any special rules below.

THE SPANISH LANGUAGE

There are almost 350 million speakers of Spanish worldwide – it is the third most widely spoken language after Chinese and English. These are the countries where you can expect to hear Spanish spoken (figures are approximate):

España Spain
Spanish is spoken by almost the entire population (40 million). Other languages: Catalan in northeastern Spain (6m), Galician in northwestern Spain (3m) and Basque (almost 1m).

México Mexico
Spanish is spoken by most of the 98 million population. Other languages: 6 million speak Indian languages, esp. Nahuatl (1.5 m), Maya (1m) in Yucatán.

América del Sur South America
Spanish is spoken by the great majority in **Argentina** (34 million); **Bolivia** (less than half the 7.5m population), other languages: Quechua (2m), Aymara (1.5m); **Colombia** (35m), other: Arawak, Carib; **Ecuador** (11m), other: Quechua (0.5m); **Paraguay** - three-quarters of the 5.5m population, other: Guarani (3m); **Peru** (24m) other: Quechua (5m), Aymara (0.5m); **Uruguay** (3.5m); **Venezuela** (22m), other: Arawak, Carib.

América Central Central America
Spanish is spoken in **Costa Rica** (3.5 million), **Cuba** (11m), **Dominican Republic** (8m); **Puerto Rico** (4m); **El Salvador** (6m); **Guatemala** (10m), other: Quiché (1m), Cakchiquel (0.5m); **Honduras** (5.5m), other: Lenca, Carib; **Nicaragua** (4m); **Panama** (3m).

Estados Unidos United States
Spanish is spoken by approx. 18 million people, especially in Texas, New Mexico, Arizona, California, southern Florida and New York City.

África Africa
Spanish is the official language of **Equatorial Guinea** (4.5m), other: Fang. Spanish is also spoken in the Spanish zone of **Morocco**.

The Spanish alphabet is the same as English, with the addition of the tilde on the letter **ñ**. The acute accent (´) indicates stress, not a change in sound.

Some Spanish words have been incorporated into English, for example **bonanza**, **canyon**, **patio**, **plaza**, **siesta**.

Until recently in Spanish, **ch** and **ll** were treated as separate letters, alphabetically ordered after **c** and **l** respectively. Look out for this when using old telephone directories or dictionaries.

There are some differences in vocabulary and pronunciation between the Spanish spoken in Spain and that in the Americas - although each is easily understood by the other. This phrase book and dictionary is specifically geared to travelers in Spain.

CONSONANTS

Letter	Approximate pronunciation	Symbol	Example	Pronunciation
b	1. as in English	b	**bueno**	_bweno_
	2. between vowels as in English, but softer	b	**bebida**	_bebeeda_
c	1. before **e** and **i**, like *th* in *th*in	th	**centro**	_thentro_
	2. otherwise like *k* in *k*it	k	**como**	_komo_
ch	as in English	ch	**mucho**	_moocho_
d	1. as in English *d*og, but less decisive	d	**donde**	_dondeh_
	2. between vowels and at the end of a word, like *th* in *th*is	th	**usted**	_oosteth_
g	1. before **e** and **i**, like *ch* in Scottish lo*ch*	kh	**urgente**	_oorkhenteh_
	2. otherwise, like *g* in *g*et	g	**ninguno**	_neengoono_
h	always silent		**hombre**	_ombreh_
j	like *ch* in Scottish lo*ch*	kh	**bajo**	_bakho_
ll	like *lli* in mi*lli*on	l-y	**lleno**	_l-yeno_
ñ	like *ni* in o*ni*on	ñ	**señor**	_señor_
qu	like *k* in *k*ick	k	**quince**	_keentheh_
r	more strongly trilled (like a Scottish *r*), especially at the beginning of a word	r	**río**	_reeo_
rr	strongly trilled	rr	**arriba**	_arreeba_

s	1. like *s* in sa*m*e	s	**vista**	_vee_sta
	2. before **b, d, g, l, m, n**,			
	like *s* in ro*s*e	z	**mismo**	mee_z_mo
v	like *b* in *b*ad, but softer	b	**viejo**	vee_ye_kho
z	like *th* in *th*in	th	**brazo**	_bra_tho

Letters **f, k, l, m, n, p, t, x** and **y** are pronounced as in English.

VOWELS

Letter	Approximate pronunciation	Symbol	Example	Pronunciation
a	in length, between *a* in English p*a*t, and *a* in English b*a*r	a	**gracias**	_gra_theeyas
e	1. like *e* in g*e*t	e	**puedo**	_pwe_do
	2. in a syllable ending in a vowel like *e* in th*ey*	eh	**me**	meh
i	like *ee* in f*ee*t	ee	**sí**	see
o	like *o* in g*o*t	o	**dos**	dos
u	1. like *oo* in f*oo*d	oo	**una**	_oo_na
	2. silent after **g** in words like **guerra, guiso,** except where marked **ü**, as in **antigüedad**			
y	only a vowel when alone or at the end of a word, like *ee* in f*ee*t	ee	**y**	ee

Note: to aid pronunciation the phonetic transcription uses **y** where applicable between groups of vowels to indicate the sound value of *y* in y*es*.

STRESS

Stress has been indicated in the phonetic transcription: underlined letters should be pronounced with more stress (i.e. louder) than the others.

In words ending with a vowel, **-n** or **-s**, the next to last syllable is stressed, e.g. **mañana** (*ma_ña_na*); in words ending in a consonant, the last syllable is stressed, e.g. **señor** (*se_ñor_*); the acute accent (´) is used in Spanish to indicate a syllable is stressed, e.g. **río** (_ree_o).

Some Spanish words have more than one meaning; the accent mark is employed to distinguish between them, e.g.: **él** (he) and **el** (the); **sí** (yes) and **si** (if); **tú** (you) and **tu** (your).

PRONUNCIATION OF THE SPANISH ALPHABET

|---|---|---|---|---|---|
A	ah	**J**	_kho_ta	**R**	_e_rreh
B	beh	**K**	ka	**S**	_eh_seh
C	theh	**L**	_eh_leh	**T**	teh
D	deh	**M**	_e_meh	**U**	oo
E	eh	**N**	_ay_nneh	**V**	_oo_bheh
F	_eh_feh	**Ñ**	_e_nyeh	**W**	_do_bleh beh
G	kheh	**O**	oh	**X**	_e_kees
H	_a_cheh	**P**	peh	**Y**	ee _gree_yega
I	ee	**Q**	koo	**Z**	_the_ta

BASIC EXPRESSIONS

GREETINGS/APOLOGIES

ESSENTIAL	
Yes./No.	**Sí.** *see*/**No.** *no*
Okay.	**De acuerdo.** *deh akwehrdo*
Please.	**Por favor.** *por fabor*
Thank you (very much).	**(Muchas) gracias.**
	(moochas) gratheeyas

Hello./Hi!	**¡Hola!** *ola*
Good morning.	**Buenos días.** *bwenos deeyas*
Good afternoon/evening.	**Buenas tardes.** *bwenas tardes*
Good night.	**Buenas noches.** *bwenas noches*
Good-bye.	**Adiós.** *adyos*
Excuse me! *(getting attention)*	**¡Disculpe!** *deeskulpeh*
Excuse me. *(May I get past?)*	**Disculpe.** *deeskulpay*
Excuse me!/Sorry!	**¡Perdón!/¡Lo siento!** *perdon/lo seeyento*
It was an accident.	**Fue un accidente.** *fweh oon aktheedenteh*
Don't mention it.	**No hay de qué.** *no eye deh keh*
Never mind.	**No tiene importancia.** *no tyeneh eemportantheeya*

ON THE STREET
¡Hola! ¿Cómo está? *ola komo esta* *(Hi. How are you?)* **Bien gracias. ¿Y usted?** *beeyen gratheeyas ee oosteth* *(Fine. And yourself?)* **Bien gracias.** *beeyen gratheeyas (Fine . Thanks.)*

COMMUNICATION DIFFICULTIES

Do you speak English?	**¿Habla inglés?** *abla eengles*
Does anyone here speak English?	**¿Hay alguien que hable inglés?** *eye algeeyen keh ableh eengles*
I don't speak (much) Spanish.	**No hablo (mucho) español.** *no ablo (moocho) español*
Could you speak more slowly?	**¿Podría hablar más despacio?** *podreeya ablar mas despatheeyo*
Could you repeat that?	**¿Podría repetir eso?** *podreeya repeteer eso*
Excuse me? [Pardon?]	**¿Cómo?** *komo*
Sorry, I didn't catch that.	**Lo siento, no entendí eso.** *lo seeyento, no entendee eso*
What was that?	**¿Qué ha dicho?** *keh a deecho*
Could you spell it?	**¿Podría deletrearlo?** *podreeya deletrayarlo*
Please write it down.	**Escríbamelo, por favor.** *eskreebamelo por fabor*
Can you translate this for me?	**¿Podría traducirme esto?** *podreeya tradootheermeh esto*
What does this/that mean?	**¿Qué significa esto/eso?** *keh seegneefeeka esto/eso*
How do you pronounce that?	**¿Cómo se pronuncia eso?** *komo se pronoontheeya eso*
Please point to the phrase in the book.	**Por favor señáleme la frase en el libro.** *por fabor señalemeh la fraseh en el leebro*
I understand.	**Entiendo.** *enteeyendo*
I don't understand.	**No entiendo.** *no enteeyendo*
Do you understand?	**¿Entiende?** *enteeyendeh*

QUESTIONS

Questions can be formed in Spanish:

1. by a questioning intonation; often the personal pronoun is left out, both in affirmative sentences and in questions:

Hablo español.	I speak Spanish.
¿Habla español?	Do you speak Spanish?

2. by using a question word plus the inverted order:

¿Cuándo llega el tren?	When does the train arrive?

Where?

Where is it?	**¿Dónde está?** _dondeh esta_
Where are you going?	**¿Dónde vas?** _dondeh bas_
to the meeting place [point]	**en el lugar de encuentro** _en el loogar deh enkwentro_
away from me	**lejos de mí** _lekhos deh mee_
from the U.S.	**de los Estados Unidos** _deh los estados oonidos_
here	**aquí** _akee_
in the car	**en el coche** _en el kocheh_
in Spain	**en España** _en españa_
inside	**dentro** _dentro_
near the bank	**cerca del banco** _therka del banko_
next to the apples	**al lado de las manzanas** _al lado deh las manthanas_
opposite the market	**enfrente del mercado** _enfrenteh del merkado_
there	**allí** _al-yee_
to the hotel	**al hotel** _al otel_
on the left/right	**a la izquierda/derecha** _a la eethkeeyerda/derecha_
on the sidewalk	**en la acera** _en la athera_
outside the café	**fuera del café** _fwera del kafeh_
up to the traffic light	**hasta el semáforo** _asta el semaforo_

When?

When does the museum open?	**¿Cuándo abre el museo?** _kwando abray el moosayo_
When does the train arrive?	**¿Cuándo llega el tren?** _kwando l-yega el tren_
at 7 o'clock	**a las siete en punto** _a las seeyeteh en poonto_
after lunch	**después de comer** _despwes deh komer_
always	**siempre** _seeyempreh_
around midnight	**a eso de las doce de la noche** _a eso deh las dotheh deh la nocheh_
before Friday	**antes del viernes** _antes del beeyernes_
by tomorrow	**para mañana** _para mañana_
every week	**todas las semanas/cada semana** _todas las semanas/kada semana_
for 2 hours	**durante dos horas** _dooranteh dos oras_
from 9 a.m. to 6 p.m.	**de nueve de la mañana a seis de la tarde** _deh nwebeh deh la mañana a says deh la tardeh_
in 20 minutes	**dentro de veinte minutos** _dentro deh beynteh meenootos_
never	**nunca** _noonka_
not yet	**todavía no** _todabeeya no_
now	**ahora** _a-ora_
often	**a menudo** _a menoodo_
on March 8	**el ocho de marzo** _el ocho de martho_
on weekdays	**durante la semana** _dooranteh la semana_
sometimes	**a veces** _a bethes_
soon	**pronto** _pronto_
then	**entonces/luego** _entonthes/looego_
within 2 days	**dentro de dos días** _dentroa deh dos deeyas_
10 minutes ago	**hace diez minutos** _athay deeyeth meenootos_

What kind of …?

I'd like something …	**Quiero algo …** keeyero algo
It's …	**Es …** es
beautiful/ugly	**bonito/feo** boneeto/fayo
better/worse	**mejor/peor** mekhor/peyor
big/small	**grande/pequeño** grandeh/pekeño
cheap/expensive	**barato/caro** barato/karo
clean/dirty	**limpio/sucio** leempeeo/sootheeo
dark/light	**oscuro/claro** oskooro/klaro
delicious/revolting	**delicioso/asqueroso** deleetheeyoso/askeroso
early/late	**temprano/tarde** temprano/tardeh
easy/difficult	**fácil/difícil** fatheel/deefeetheel
empty/full	**vacío/lleno** batheeyo/l-yeno
good/bad	**bueno/malo** bweno/malo
heavy/light	**pesado/ligero** pesado/likhehro
hot, warm/cold	**caliente/frío** kaleeyenteh/freeyo
modern/old-fashioned	**moderno/antiguo** moderno/anteegwoa
narrow/wide	**estrecho/ancho** estrecho/ancho
next/last	**próximo/último** prokseemo/oolteemo
old/new	**viejo/nuevo** beeyekho/nwebo
open/shut	**abierto/cerrado** abeeyerto/therrado
pleasant, nice/unpleasant	**agradable/desagradable** agradableh/desagradableh
quick/slow	**rápido/lento** rrapeedo/lento
quiet/noisy	**silencioso/ruidoso** seelentheeyoso/rrooeeydoso

right/wrong	**correcto/incorrecto**	
	korrekto/eenkorrekto	
tall/short	**alto/bajo** _alto/bakho_	
thick/thin	**grueso/fino** _grooeso/feeno_	
vacant/occupied	**libre/ocupado** _leebreh/okoopado_	
young/old	**joven/viejo** _khoben/beeyekho_	

How much/many?

How much is this/that?	**¿Cuánto es esto/eso?** _kwanto es esto/eso_
How many are there?	**¿Cuántos hay?** _kwantos eye_
1/2/3	**uno/dos/tres** _oono/dos/tres_
4/5	**cuatro/cinco** _kwatro/theenko_
none	**ninguno** _neengoono_
about 20 euros	**unos veinte euros**
	oonos baynteh eh-ooros
a little	**un poco** _oon poko_
a lot of traffic	**mucho tráfico** _moocho trafeeko_
enough	**bastante** _bastanteh_
few	**pocos(-as)** _pokos(-as)_
a few of them	**unos(-as) pocos(-as)** _oonos(-as) pokos(-as)_
many people	**mucha gente** _moocha khenteh_
more than that	**más que eso** _mas keh eso_
less than that	**menos que eso** _menos keh eso_
much more	**mucho más** _moocho mas_
nothing else	**nada más** _nada mas_
too much	**demasiado** _demaseeyado_

Why?

Why is that?	**¿Por qué?** _por keh_
Why not?	**¿Por qué no?** _por keh no_
because of the weather	**por el tiempo** _por el teeyempo_
because I'm in a hurry	**porque tengo prisa**
	porkeh tengo preesa
I don't know why.	**No sé por qué.** _no seh por keh_

Who?/Which?

Who's there?	**¿Quién es?** *keeyen es*
Who is it for?	**¿Para quién es?** *para keeyen es*
either ... or ...	**o ... o ...** *o... o*
her/him	**ella/él** *el-ya/el*
me	**mí** *mee*
you	**ti** *tee*
them	**ellos** *el-yos*
someone	**alguien** *algeeyen*
none/no one	**ninguno/nadie** *neengoono/nadeeay*
Which one do you want?	**¿Cuál quiere?** *kwal keeyereh*
that one/this one	**ése/éste** *eseh/esteh*
not that one	**ése no** *eseh no*
one like that	**uno como ése** *oono komo eseh*
something	**algo** *algo*

Whose?

Whose is that?	**¿De quién es eso?** *deh keeyehn es eso*
It's mine/ours.	**Es el mío/el nuestro.** *es el meeyo/el nwestro*
yours	**suyo/tuyo/vuestro** *sooyo/tooyo/bwestro*
his/hers/theirs	**suyo** *sooyo*
It's ... turn.	**Es ... turno.** *es ... toorno*
my/our	**mi/nuestro** *mee/nwestro*
your	**su/tu/vuestro** *soo/too/bwestro*
his/her/their	**su** *soo*

How?

How would you like to pay?	**¿Cómo le gustaría pagar?** _komo le goostareeya pagar_
How are you getting here?	**¿Cómo va a venir aquí?** _komo bas a beneer akee_
by car	**en coche** _en kocheh_
by credit card	**con tarjeta de crédito** _kon tarkheta deh kredeeto_
by chance	**por casualidad** _por kasooalidath_
equally	**igualmente** _eegwalmenteh_
extremely	**sumamente** _soomamente_
on foot	**a pie** _a peeyeh_
quickly	**rápidamente** _rapeedamenteh_
slowly	**despacio** _despatheeyo_
too fast	**demasiado deprisa** _demaseeyado depreesa_
totally	**totalmente** _totalmenteh_
very	**muy** _mwee_
with a friend	**con un(a) amigo(a)** _kon un(a) ameego(a)_
without a passport	**sin pasaporte** _seen pasaporteh_

Is it …?/Are there …?

Is it …?	**¿Es/está …?** _es/esta_
Is it free of charge?	**¿Es gratis?** _es gratees_
It isn't ready.	**No está listo.** _no esta leesto_
Is/Are there …?	**¿Hay …?** _eye_
Are there any buses into town?	**¿Hay autobúses para ir a la ciudad?** _eye aootobooses para eer a la theeoodath_
There are showers in the rooms.	**Hay duchas en las habitaciones.** _eye doochas en las abeetatheeyones_
Here it is/they are.	**Aquí tiene/los tiene.** _akee teeyeneh/los teeyeneh_
There it is/they are.	**Ahí está/están.** _ahee esta/estan_

Can … ?

Can I have …?	**¿Puedo tomar …?** *pwedo tomar*
Can we have …?	**¿Podemos tomar …?** *podemos tomar*
Can you show me …?	**¿Puede enseñarme …?** *pwedeh enseñarmeh*
Can you tell me?	**¿Puede decirme?** *pwedeh detheermeh*
Can you help me?	**¿Puede ayudarme?** *pwedeh ayoodarmeh*
Can I help you?	**¿Puedo ayudarle?** *pwedo ayoodarleh*
Can you direct me to …?	**¿Puede indicarme cómo ir a …?** *pwede eendeekarmeh komo eer a*
I can't.	**No puedo.** *no pwedo*

What do you want?

I'd like …	**Quiero …** *keeyero*
Could I have …?	**¿Podría tomar …?** *podreeya tomar*
We'd like …	**Queremos …** *keremos*
Give me …	**Déme …** *demeh*
I'm looking for …	**Estoy buscando …** *estoy booskando*
I need to …	**Necesito …** *netheseeto*
go …	**ir …** *eer*
find …	**encontrar …** *enkontrar*
see …	**ver …** *behr*
speak to …	**hablar con …** *ablar kon*

IN THE POST OFFICE

¿De quién es este bolso? *deh keeyehn es este bolso*
(Whose handbag is that?)
Es el mío. Gracias. *es el meeyo gratheeyas*
(It's mine. Thanks.)
De nada. *de nada (You're welcome.)*

OTHER USEFUL WORDS

fortunately	**afortunadamente** *afortoonadamenteh*
hopefully	**con algo de suerte** *kon algo deh swerteh*
of course	**por supuesto** *por soopwesto*
perhaps	**quizás** *keetha*
unfortunately	**desgraciadamente** *desgratheeyadamenteh*
also	**también** *tambeeyen*
and	**y** *ee*
but	**pero** *pero*
or	**o** *o*

EXCLAMATIONS

And so on.	**Etcétera, etcétera.** *etthetera etthetera*
At last!	**¡Por fin!** *por feen*
Carry on.	**Continúa.** *konteenooa*
Nonsense.	**Tonterías.** *tontereeyas*
Quite right too!	**¡Puedes estar seguro(-a)!** *pwedes estar segooro(-a)*
You're joking!	**¡No me digas!** *no meh deegas*
How are things?	**¿Cómo te va?** *komo teh ba*
great/brilliant	**estupendamente** *estoopendamenteh*
great	**muy bien** *mwee beeyen*
fine/okay	**bien** *beeyen*
not bad	**no demasiado mal** *no demaseeyado mal*
not good	**no muy bien** *no mwee beeyen*
fairly bad	**bastante mal** *bastanteh mal*
terrible	**fatal** *fatal.*

ACCOMMODATIONS

All types of accommodations, from hotels to campsites, can be found through the tourist information center (**Oficina de turismo**).

Early reservations are essential in most major tourist centers, especially during high season or special events. If you haven't booked, you're more likely to find accommodations available outside towns and city centers.

Hotel *otel*
There are five official categories of hotels: luxury, first class A, first class B, second class and third class. There may be price variations within any given category, depending on the location and the facilities offered. There are also, of course, plenty of unclassified hotels where you will find clean, simple accommodations and good food.

Refugio *refookhyo*
Small inns in remote and mountainous regions. They are often closed in winter.

Albergue de juventud *albergeh deh khoobentooth*
Youth hostel. There is usually no age limit; become a member and your **carnet de alberguista** will entitle you to a discount. There isn't an extensive network in Spain, but **casas de huéspedes** (**CH**) and **fondas** (**F**) provide budget-conscious alternatives.

Apartamento amueblado *apartamento amweblado*
A furnished apartment (flat) mainly in resorts. Available from specialized travel agents or directly from the landlord (look for the sign **se alquila** – for rent, to let).

Hostal *ostal*
Modest hotels, often family concerns, graded one to three stars; denoted by the sign **Hs**.

Parador *parador*
Palaces, country houses or castles that have been converted into hotels and are under government supervision. Their aim is to provide the chance to experience "the real Spain." The central reservation agency is **Paradores de España** ☎ 435 97 00.

Pensión *pensyon*
Boardinghouses, graded one to three stars; denoted by the sign **P**.

RESERVATIONS/BOOKING

In advance

Can you recommend a hotel in …?	**¿Puede recomendarme un hotel en …?** *pwede rekomendarmeh oon otel en*
Is it near the center (of town)?	**¿Está cerca del centro (de la ciudad)?** *esta therka del thentro (deh la theeyoodath)*
How much is it per night?	**¿Cuánto cuesta por noche?** *kwanto kwesta por nocheh*
Is there anything cheaper?	**¿Hay algo más barato?** *eye algo mas barato*
Could you reserve me a room there, please?	**¿Podría reservarme una habitación allí por favor?** *podreeya reserbarmeh oona abeetatheeyon al-yee por fabor*
How do I get there?	**¿Cómo llego allí?** *komo l-yego al-yee*

At the hotel

Do you have a room?	**¿Tienen habitaciones libres?** *teeyenen abeetatheeyones leebres*
Is there another hotel nearby?	**¿Hay otro hotel por aquí cerca?** *eye otro otel por akee therka*
I'd like a single/double room.	**Quiero una habitación individual/doble.** *keeyero oona abeetatheeyon eendeebeedooal/dobleh*
A room with …	**Una habitación con …** *oona abeetatheeyon kon*
a double bed/twin beds	**una cama de matrimonio/dos camas** *oona kama deh matreemoneeyo/dos kamas*
a bath/shower	**un baño/una ducha** *oon baño/oona doocha*

AT THE HOTEL RECEPTION

¿Tienen habitaciones libres? *teeyenen abeetatheeyones leebres* (*Do you have any vacancies?*)
Lo siento. *lo seeyento* (*I'm sorry.*)
Gracias. Adiós. *gratheeyas adyos* (*Thank you. Good bye.*)

RECEPTION

I have a reservation. My name is …	**Tengo una reserva. Me llamo …** *tengo oona reserba. meh l-yamo*
We've reserved a double and a single room.	**Hemos reservado una habitación doble y una individual.** *emos reserbado oona abeetatheeyon dobleh ee oona eendeebeedooal*
I confirmed my reservation by mail.	**Confirmé mi reserva por carta.** *konfeermeh mee reserba por karta*
Could we have adjoining rooms?	**¿Nos podrían dar habitaciones conjuntas?** *nos podreeyan dar abeetatheeyones konkhoontas*

Amenities and facilities

Is there (a) … in the room?	**¿Hay (un/una) … en la habitación?** *eye (oon/oona) … en la abeetatheeyon*
air conditioning	**aire acondicionado** *ayray akondeethyonado*
TV/telephone	**televisión/teléfono** *telebeeseeyon/telefono*
Does the hotel have (a)…?	**¿Tiene el hotel (un/una) …?** *teeyeneh el otel (oon/oona)*
fax facilities	**fax** *fax*
laundry service	**servicio de lavandería** *serbeetheeyo deh labandereeya*
satellite TV	**antena parabólica** *antena paraboleeka*
sauna	**sauna** *saoona*
swimming pool	**piscina** *peestheena*
Could you put … in the room?	**¿Podrían poner … en la habitación?** *podreean poner … en la abeetatheeyon*
an extra bed	**otra cama** *otra kama*
a crib/child's cot	**una cuna** *oona koona*
Do you have facilities for …?	**¿Tienen instalaciones para …?** *teeyenen eenstalatheeyones para*
the disabled/children	**los minusválidos/niños** *los meenusbaleedos/neeños*

How long?

We'll be staying …	**Nos quedaremos …** _nos kedaremos_
overnight only	**sólo esta noche** _solo esta nocheh_
a few days	**unos días** _oonos deeyas_
a week (at least)	**una semana (por lo menos)** _oona semana (por lo menos)_
I'd like to stay an extra night.	**Quiero quedarme una noche más.** _keeyero kedarmeh oona nocheh mas_
What does this mean?	**¿Qué significa esto?** _keh seegneefeeka esto_

IN THE STORE

¿Cómo le gustaría pagar? _komo le goostareeya pagar_
(How would you like to pay?)
En metálico, por favor. _en metaleeko por fabor_
(Cash, please.)

YOU MAY HEAR

¿Puedo ver su pasaporte?	May I see your passport?
Rellene este formulario/ firme aquí, por favor.	Please fill out this form/sign here.
¿Cuál es su número de matrícula?	What is your license plate [registration] number?

YOU MAY SEE

DESAYUNO INCLUIDO	breakfast included
SE DAN COMIDAS	meals available
SÓLO LA HABITACIÓN … EUROS	room only … euros
APELIDO/NOMBRE	name/first name
DOMICILIO/CALLE/NÚMERO	home address/street/number
NACIONALIDAD/PROFESIÓN	nationality/profession
FECHA/LUGAR DE NACIMIENTO	date/place of birth
NÚMERO DE PASAPORTE	passport number
NÚMERO DE MATRÍCULA	license plate [registration]number
LUGAR/FECHA	place/date
FIRMA	signature

Prices

How much is it …?	**¿Cuánto es …?** _kwanto es_
per night/week	**por noche/semana** _por nocheh/semana_
for bed and breakfast	**por desayuno y habitación** _por desayoono ee abeetatheeyon_
excluding meals	**excluyendo las comidas** _exklooyendo las komeedas_
for full board (American Plan [A.P.])	**por pensión completa** _por penseeyon kompleta_
for half board (Modified American Plan [M.A.P.])	**por media pensión** _por medeeya penseeyon_
Does the price include …?	**¿Incluye el precio …?** _eenklooyeh el pretheeo_
breakfast	**el desayuno** _el desayoono_
service	**el servicio** _el serbeetheeo_
sales tax [VAT]	**IVA** _eeba_
Do I have to pay a deposit?	**¿Tengo que pagar un depósito?** _tengo keh pagar oon deposeeto_
Is there a reduction for children?	**¿Hay un descuento para los niños?** _eye oon deskwento para los neeños_

Decisions

May I see the room?	**¿Puedo ver la habitación?** _pwedo behr la abeetatheeyon_
That's fine. I'll take it.	**Está bien. Me la quedo.** _esta beeyen. meh la kedo_
It's too …	**Es demasiado …** _es demaseeyado_
dark/small	**oscura/pequeña** _oskoora/pekeña_
noisy	**ruidosa** _rooeedosa_
Do you have anything …?	**¿Tiene algo …?** _teeyeneh algo_
bigger/cheaper	**más grande/más barato** _mas grandeh/mas barato_
quieter/warmer	**más tranquilo/menos frío** _mas trankeelo/menos freeyo_
No, I won't take it.	**No, no me quedo con ella.** _no, no meh kedo kon el-ya_

PROBLEMS

The … doesn't work.	**… no funciona.**	no foontheeyona
air conditioning	**el aire acondicionado**	el ayreh akondeetheeyonado
fan	**el ventilador**	el benteelador
heat	**la calefacción**	la kalefaktheeyon
light	**la luz**	la looth
I can't turn the heat [heating] on/off.	**No puedo encender/apagar la calefacción.**	no pwedo enthender/apagar la kalefaktheeyon
There is no hot water/ toilet paper.	**No hay agua caliente/papel higiénico.**	no eye agwa kaleeyenteh/papel eekheeyeneeko
The faucet [tap] is dripping.	**El grifo gotea.**	el greefo goteya
The sink/toilet is blocked.	**El lavabo/wáter está atascado.**	el lababo/bater esta ataskado
The window/door is jammed.	**La ventana/puerta está atascada.**	la bentana/pwerta esta ataskada
My room has not been made up.	**No han hecho la habitación.**	no an echo la abeetatheeyon
The … is broken.	**… está roto(-a).**	… esta roto(-a)
blind/shutter	**la persiana**	la perseeyana
lamp	**la lámpara**	la lampara
lock	**el pestillo**	el pesteel-yo
There are insects in our room.	**Hay insectos en nuestra habitación.**	eye eensektos en nwestra abeetatheeyon

Action

Could you have that taken care of?	**¿Podrían encargarse de eso?**	podreeyan enkargarseh deh eso
I'd like to move to another room.	**Quiero mudarme a otra habitación.**	keeyero mudarmeh a otra abeetatheeyon
I'd like to speak to the manager.	**Quiero hablar con el gerente.**	keeyero ablar kon el kherenteh

REQUIREMENTS

The 220-volt, 50-cycle AC is the norm throughout Spain. If you bring your own electrical appliances, buy a Continental adapter plug (round pins, not square) before leaving home. You may also need a transformer appropriate to the wattage of the appliance.

About the hotel

Where's the …?	**¿Dónde está …?** _dondeh esta_
bar	**el bar** _el bar_
bathroom	**el cuarto de baño** _el kwarto deh baño_
restroom [toilet]	**el servicio** _el serbeetheeyo_
dining room	**el comedor** _el komedor_
elevator	**el ascensor** _el asthensor_
parking lot [car park]	**el aparcamiento** _el aparkameeyento_
shower	**la ducha** _la doocha_
swimming pool	**la piscina** _la peestheena_
tour operator's bulletin board	**el tablón de anuncios del operador turístico** _el tablon deh anoontheeyos del operador tooreesteeko_
Does the hotel have a garage?	**¿Tiene garaje el hotel?** _teeyeneh garakheh el otel_
Can I use this adapter here?	**¿Puedo utilizar este adaptador aquí?** _pwedo ooteeleethar esteh adaptador akee_

YOU MAY SEE

MARQUE … PARA HABLAR CON RECEPCIÓN	dial … for reception
MARQUE … PARA UNA LÍNEA EXTERIOR	dial … for an outside line
NO MOLESTAR	do not disturb
PROHIBIDO COMER EN LA HABITACIÓN	no food in the room
PUERTA DE INCENDIOS	fire door
SALIDA DE EMERGENCIA	emergency exit
SÓLO PARA UTILIZAR MÁQUINAS DE AFEITAR	razors [shavers] only

Personal needs

The key to room …, please.	**La llave de la habitación…, por favor.** *la l-yabeh dehla abeetatheeyon … por fabor*
I've lost my key.	**He perdido la llave.** *eh perdeedo la l-yabeh*
I've locked myself out of my room.	**No puedo entrar en mi habitación.** *no pwedo entrar en mee abeetatheeyon*
Could you wake me at …?	**¿Podría despertarme a la/las …?** *podreeya despertarmeh a la/las*
I'd like breakfast in my room.	**Quiero que me traigan el desayuno a la habitación.** *keeyero keh meh traygan el desayoono a la abeetatheeyon*
Can I leave this in the safe?	**¿Puedo dejar esto en la caja fuerte?** *pwedo dekhar esto en la kakha fwerteh*
Could I have my things from the safe?	**¿Podría darme mis cosas de la caja fuerte?** *podreeya darmeh mees kosas de la kakha fwerteh*
Where can I find (a) …?	**¿Dónde puedo encontrar a …?** *dondeh pwedo enkontrar a*
maid	**la chica del servicio** *la cheeka del serbeethyo*
our tour representative	**nuestro representante turístico** *nwestro representanteh tooreestiko*
Can I have (a) …?	**¿Pueden darme …?** *pweden darmeh*
bath towel	**una toalla de baño** *oona toayl-ya deh baño*
blanket	**una manta** *oona manta*
hangers	**perchas** *perchas*
pillow	**una almohada** *oona almoada*
soap	**jabón** *khabon*
Is there any mail for me?	**¿Hay correo para mí?** *eye korreho para mee*
Are there any messages for me?	**¿Hay algún mensaje para mí?** *eye algoon mensakheh para mee*

RENTING

We've reserved an apartment.	**Hemos reservado un apartamento.** *emos reserbado oon apartamento*
in the name of …	**a nombre de …** *a nombreh deh*
Where do we pick up the keys?	**¿Dónde recogemos las llaves?** *dondeh rekokhemos las l-yabes*
Where is the…?	**¿Dónde está …?** *dondeh esta*
electric meter	**el contador de la luz** *el kontador deh la looth*
fuse box	**la caja de fusibles** *la kakha deh fooseebles*
valve [stopcock]	**la llave de paso** *la l-yabeh deh paso*
water heater	**el calentador** *el kalentador*
Are there any spare …?	**¿Hay … de repuesto?** *eye … deh repwesto*
fuses	**fusibles** *fooseebles*
fuses/gas bottles	**bombonas de gas butano** *bombonas deh gas bootano*
sheets	**sábanas** *sabanas*
Which day does the maid come?	**¿Qué día viene la limpiadora?** *keh deeya beeyeneh la leempeeadora*
When do I put out the trash [rubbish]?	**¿Cuándo hay que sacar la basura?** *kwando eye keh sakar la basoora*

Problems?

Where can I contact you?	**¿Dónde me puedo poner en contacto con usted?** *dondeh meh pwedo poner en kontakto kon oosteth*
How does the stove [cooker]/water heater work?	**¿Cómo funciona la cocina/el calentador?** *komo foontheeyona la kotheena/el kalentador*
The … is/are dirty.	**… está/están sucios.** *esta/estan sootheeyos*
The … has broken down.	**… se ha estropeado.** *seh a estropeyado*
We accidentally broke/lost …	**Hemos roto/perdido … sin querer.** *emos roto/perdeedo … seen kerer*
That was already damaged when we arrived.	**Eso ya estaba estropeado cuando llegamos.** *eso ya estaba estropeado kwando l-yegamos*

Useful terms

dishes [crockery]	**la vajilla**	*la bakheel-ya*
freezer	**el congelador**	*el konkhelador*
frying pan	**la sartén**	*la sarten*
kettle	**el hervidor**	*el erbeedor*
lamp	**la lámpara**	*la lampara*
refrigerator	**el frigorífico**	*el freegoreefeeko*
saucepan	**el cazo**	*el katho*
stove [cooker]	**la cocina**	*la kotheena*
utensils [cutlery]	**los cubiertos**	*los koobeeyertos*
washing machine	**la lavadora**	*la labadora*

Rooms

balcony	**el balcón**	*el balkon*
bathroom	**el cuarto de baño**	*el kwarto deh baño*
bedroom	**el dormitorio**	*el dormeetoreeyo*
dining room	**el comedor**	*el komedor*
kitchen	**la cocina**	*la kotheena*
living room	**el salón/la sala de estar**	*el salon/la sala deh estar*
toilet	**el servicio**	*el serbeetheeyo*

YOUTH HOSTEL

Youth hostels in Spain are few and far between, though a list is available from the Spanish National Tourist Office.

Do you have any places left for tonight?	**¿Tiene algún lugar libre para esta noche?** *teeyeneh algoon loogar leebreh para esta nocheh*
Do you rent out bedding?	**¿Alquilan ropa de cama?** *alkeelan ropa deh kama*
What time are the doors locked?	**¿A qué hora cierran las puertas?** *a keh ora theeyeran las pwertas*
I have an International Student Card.	**Tengo el carnet internacional de estudiante.** *tengo el karnet eenternatheeyonal deh estoodeeanteh*

CAMPING

Spanish campsites are categorized luxury, 1st, 2nd or 3rd class. Facilities vary, but all have toilets, showers, drinking water and 24-hour surveillance. For a complete list of campsites, facilities and rates contact any Spanish National Tourist Office.

Reservations

Is there a campsite near here?	**¿Hay un cámping cerca de aquí?** *eye oon kampeen therka deh akee*
Do you have space for a tent/trailer [caravan]?	**¿Tienen una parcela para una tienda/ roulotte?** *teeyenen oona parthela para oona teeyenda/roolot*
What is the charge …?	**¿Cuánto cobran …?** *kwanto kobran*
per day/week	**por día/semana** *por deeya/semana*
for a tent/a car	**por tienda/por coche** *por teeyenda/por kocheh*
for a trailer [caravan]	**por roulotte** *por roolot*

Facilities

Are there cooking facilities on site?	**¿Tienen instalaciones para cocinar en el recinto?** *teeyenen eenstalatheeyones para kotheenar en el retheento*
Are there any electric outlets [power points]?	**¿Hay enchufes eléctricos?** *eye enshoofez elektreekos*
Where is/are the …?	**¿Dónde está/están …?** *dondeh esta/estan*
drinking water	**el agua potable** *el agwa potableh*
trash cans [dustbins]	**las papeleras** *las papeleras*
laundry facilities	**el servicio de lavandería** *el serbeetheeyo deh labandereeya*
showers	**las duchas** *las doochas*
Where can I get some butane gas?	**¿Dónde puedo comprar gas butano?** *dondeh pwedo komprar gas bootano*

YOU MAY SEE

AGUA POTABLE	drinking water
PROHIBIDO ACAMPAR	no camping
PROHIBIDO HACER HOGUERAS/BARBACOAS	no fires/barbecues

Complaints

It's too sunny here.	**Hay demasiado sol aquí.** *eye demaseeyado sol akee*
It's too shady/crowded here.	**Hay demasiada sombra/gente aquí.** *eye demaseeyada sombra/khenteh akee*
The ground's too hard/uneven.	**El suelo está demasiado duro/desnivelado.** *el swelo esta demaseeyado dooro/desneebelado*
Do you have a more level spot?	**¿Tiene una parcela más nivelada?** *teeyeneh oona parthela mas neebelada*
You can't camp here.	**No puede acampar aquí.** *no pwedeh akampar akee*

Camping equipment

butane gas	**el gas butano** *el gas bootano*
campbed	**la cama de cámping** *la kama deh kampeen*
charcoal	**el carbón** *el karbon*
flashlight [torch]	**la linterna** *la leenterna*
groundcloth [groundsheet]	**el aislante para el suelo** *el ayslanteh para el swelo*
guy rope	**la cuerda tensora** *la kwerda tensora*
hammer	**el martillo** *el marteel-yo*
kerosene [primus] stove	**el hornillo de queroseno** *el orneel-yo deh keroseno*
knapsack	**la mochila** *la mocheela*
mallet	**el mazo** *el matho*
matches	**las cerillas** *las thereel-yas*
(air) mattress	**el colchón (inflable)** *el kolchon (eenflableh)*
sleeping bag	**el saco de dormir** *el sako deh dormeer*
tent	**la tienda** *la teeyenda*
tent pegs	**las estacas** *las estakas*
tent pole	**el mástil** *el masteel*

31

CHECKING OUT

What time do we need to vacate the room?	**¿A qué hora tenemos que desocupar la habitación?** *a keh ora tenemos keh des-okoopar la abeetatheeyon*
Could we leave our baggage here until …?	**¿Podríamos dejar nuestro equipaje aquí hasta las …?** *podreeyamos dekhar nwestro ekeepakheh akee asta las …*
I'm leaving now.	**Me voy ahora.** *meh boy a-ora*
Could you call me a taxi, please?	**¿Me podría pedir un taxi, por favor?** *meh podreeya pedeer oon taksee por fabor*
I/We've had a very enjoyable stay.	**He/Hemos disfrutado mucho nuestra estancia.** *eh/emos deesfrootado moocho nwestra estantheeya*

Paying

May I have my bill, please?	**¿Me da la cuenta, por favor?** *meh da la kwenta, por fabor*
How much is my telephone bill?	**¿Cuánto es la cuenta de teléfono?** *kwanto es la kwenta deh telefono*
I think there's a mistake on this bill.	**Creo que hay un error en esta cuenta.** *krayo keh eye oon error en esta kwenta*
I've made … telephone calls.	**He hecho … llamadas.** *eh echo … l-yamadas*
I've taken … from the mini-bar.	**He tomado … del minibar.** *eh tomado … del meeneebar*
Can I have an itemized bill?	**¿Pueden darme una cuenta detallada?** *pweden darmeh oona kwenta detal-yada*

Tipping

A service charge is generally included in hotel and restaurant bills. However, if the service has been particularly good, you may want to leave an extra tip. The following chart is a guide:

	Suggested tip
Bellman	€1–2
Hotel maid, for extra services	€2–3
Waiter	10% up to €10 then 5%

EATING OUT

RESTAURANTS

Bar *bar*
Bar; drinks and tapas served, sometimes hot beverages too.

Café *kafeh*
Cafés can be found on virtually every street corner. An indispensable part of everyday life, the café is where people get together for a chat over a coffee, soft drink or glass of wine.

Cafetería *kafetereeya*
Coffee shop; there's counter service or – for a small amount more – you can choose a table. Fast food is generally served and the set menu is often very good.

Casa de comidas *kassa deh komeedass*
Simple inn serving cheap meals.

Heladería *eladereeya*
Ice cream parlor

Merendero *merendero*
Cheap open-air bar; you can usually eat outdoors.

Parador *parador*
A government-supervised establishment located in a historic castle, palace or former monastery. A parador is usually noted for excellent regional dishes served in a dining room with handsome Spanish decor.

Venta *benta*
Restaurant; often specializing in regional cooking.

Pastelería/Confitería *pastelereeya/konfeetereeya*
Pastry shop; some serve coffee, tea and drinks.

Posada *possada*
A simple inn; the food is usually simple but good.

Refugio *refookhyo*
Mountain lodge serving simple meals.

Restaurante *restowranteh*
Restaurant; these are classified by the government but the official rating has more to do with the decor than with the quality of cooking.

Salón de té *salon deh teh*
Tearoom; an upmarket cafeteria.

Taberna *taberna*
Similar to an English pub or American tavern in atmosphere; always a variety of tapas on hand as well as other snacks.

Tasca *taska*
Similar to a bar; drinks and tapas are served at the counter; standing only.

Meal times

el desayuno *el dessayoono*
Breakfast: generally from 7 to 10 a.m, traditionally toast/roll and coffee; hotels are now offering fare for tourists, serving a buffet breakfast.

la comida *la komeedah*
Lunch is generally served from around 2 or 3 p.m. The Spaniards like to linger over a meal, so service may seem on the leisurely side. In a hurry, go for fast-food outlets, pizzerias or cafés.

la merienda *la maryendah*
Light meal between 5-6pm to hold you up until dinner.

la cena *la theyna*
Dinner is served from 8.30 p.m. (10 p.m. in Madrid) to 11 p.m. However, in tourist areas you can get a meal at most places just about any time of day.

SPANISH CUISINE

The variety of Spanish cuisine comes from Celtic, Roman, Arab and New World influences, together with the profusion of Atlantic and Mediterranean seafood.

Most restaurants will offer a good value daily special (**menú del día**) – usually a three-course meal with house wine at a set price. Service and taxes are always included in the price.

ESSENTIAL	
A table for ..., please.	**Una mesa para ..., por favor.**
	oona mesa para ..., por fabor
1/2/3/4	**uno/dos/tres/cuatro**
	oono/dos/tres/kwatro
Thank you.	**Gracias.** *gratheeyas*
The bill, please.	**La cuenta, por favor.**
	la kwenta por fabor

FINDING A PLACE TO EAT

Can you recommend a good restaurant?	**¿Puede recomendarme un buen restaurante?** _pwedeh rekomendarmeh oon bwen restawranteh_
Is there (a/an) … near here?	**¿Hay … cerca de aquí?** _eye … therka deh akee_
Chinese restaurant	**un restaurante chino** _oon restawranteh cheeno_
Greek restaurant	**un restaurante griego** _oon restawranteh greeyego_
inexpensive restaurant	**un restaurante barato** _oon restawranteh barato_
Italian restaurant	**un restaurante italiano** _oon restawranteh eetaleeyano_
traditional local restaurant	**un restaurante típico** _oon restawranteh teepeeko_
vegetarian restaurant	**un restaurante vegetariano** _oon restawranteh bekhetareeyano_
Where can I find a(n) …?	**¿Dónde puedo encontrar …?** _dondeh pwedo enkontrar_
burger stand	**una hamburguesería** _oona amboorgesereeya_
café/restaurant with a garden	**una cafetería/un restaurante con jardín** _oona kafetereeya/oon restawranteh kon khardeen_
fast food restaurant	**un restaurante de comida rápida** _oon restawranteh deh komeeda rapeeda_
ice cream parlor	**una heladería** _oona eladereeya_
pizzeria	**una pizzería** _oona peethereeya_
steak house	**una churrasquería** _oona choorraskereeya_

35

RESERVING A TABLE

I'd like to reserve a table …	**Quiero reservar una mesa …** *keeyero reserbar oona mesa*
for 2	**para dos** *para dos*
for this evening/tomorrow at …	**para esta noche/mañana a las …** *para esta nocheh/mañana a las*
We'll come at 8:00.	**Llegaremos a las 8:00.** *l-yegaremos a las ocho*
A table for 2, please.	**Una mesa para dos, por favor.** *oona mesa para dos por fabor*
We have a reservation.	**Tenemos una reserva.** *tenemos oona reserba*

Where to sit

Could we sit …?	**¿Podríamos sentarnos …?** *podreeyamos sentarnos*
over there/outside	**allí/fuera** *al-yee/fwera*
in a non-smoking area	**en una zona de no fumadores** *en oona thona deh no foomadores*
by the window	**al lado de la ventana** *al lado deh la bentana*

YOU MAY HEAR

¿Van a pedir ya?	Are you ready to order?
¿Qué va a tomar?	What would you like?
¿Quieren beber algo primero?	Would you like to order drinks first?
Le recomiendo …	I recommend …
Eso tardará … minutos.	That will take … minutes.
Que aproveche.	Enjoy your meal.

Ordering

Waiter/Waitress!	**¡Camarero/Camarera!** _kamarero/kamarera_
May I see the wine list?	**¿Puedo ver la carta de vinos?** _pwedo behr la karta deh beenos_
Do you have a set menu?	**¿Tienen un menú del día?** _teeyenen oon menoo del deeya_
Can you recommend some typical local dishes?	**¿Puede recomendarme algunos platos típicos de la zona?** _pwede rekomendarmeh algoonos platos teepeekos deh la thona_
Could you tell me what … is?	**¿Podría decirme lo que … es?** _podreeya detheermeh lo keh … es_
What's in it?	**¿Qué lleva?** _keh l-yeba_
What kind of … do you have?	**¿Qué clase de … tiene?** _keh klaseh deh … teeyeneh_
I'll have …	**Tomaré …** _tomareh_
a bottle/glass/carafe of …	**una botella/un vaso/una garrafa de …** _oona botel-ya/oon baso/oona garrafa deh_

IN A RESTAURANT

La cuenta, por favor. _la kwenta por fabor_ (The bill please.)
Aquí tiene. _akee teeyeneh_ (Here you are.)
Gracias. _gratheeyas_ (Thanks.)

Side dishes/Accompaniments

Could I have … without …?	**¿Podrían servirme … sin …?** *podreeyan serbeermeh … seen*
With a side order of …	**De guarnición …** *deh gwarneetheeyon*
I'd like … as a starter/ main course/side order.	**Quiero … de primero/segundo/guarnición.** *keeyero … deh preemero/segoondo/ gwarneetheeyon*
Could I have salad instead of vegetables, please?	**¿Podría tomar ensalada en lugar de verduras, por favor?** *podreeya tomar ensalada en loogar de berdooras por fabor*
Does the meal come with vegetables/potatoes?	**¿Viene la comida con verduras/patatas?** *beeyeneh la komeeda kon berdooras/patatas*
Do you have any …?	**¿Tienen …?** *teeyenen*
bread/mayonnaise	**pan/mayonesa** *pan/mayonesa*
I'd like … with that.	**Quiero … con eso.** *keeyero … kon eso*
vegetables/salad	**verduras/ensalada** *berdooras/ensalada*
potatoes/fries [chips]/rice	**patatas/patatas fritas/arroz** *patatas/patatas freetas/arroth*
sauce	**salsa** *salsa*
ice	**hielo** *eeyelo*
May I have some …?	**¿Me puede traer …?** *me pwedeh trayer*
butter	**mantequilla** *mantekeel-ya*
lemon	**limón** *leemon*
mustard	**mostaza** *mostatha*
pepper	**pimienta** *peemeeyenta*
salt	**sal** *sal*
seasoning	**aderezo** *aderetho*
sugar	**azúcar** *athookar*
artificial sweetener	**edulcorante artificial** *edoolkorante arteefeetheeyal*
blue cheese dressing	**salsa de queso azul** *salsa deh keso athool*
vinaigrette [French dressing]	**vinagreta/vinagreta francesa** *beenagreta/ beenagreta franthesa*

General questions

Could I have a(n)
(clean) …, please?

¿Podría traerme … (limpio/a), por favor?
*podreeya trayerme … (leempeeyo/a)
por fabor*

cup/glass

una taza/un vaso *oona tatha/oon baso*

fork/knife

un tenedor/cuchillo
oon tenedor/koocheel-yo

napkin

una servilleta *oona serbeel-yeta*

plate/spoon

una plato/una cuchara
oona plato/oona koochara

I'd like some
more …, please.

Quiero más …, por favor.
keeyero mas … por fabor

Nothing more, thanks.

Nada más, gracias.
nada mas gratheeyas

Where are the restrooms
[toilets]?

¿Dónde están los servicios? *dondeh estan
los serbeetheeyos*

Special requirements

I mustn't eat food
containing …

No debo comer comida que tenga …
no debo komer komeeda keh tenga …

salt/sugar

sal/azúcar *sal/athookar*

Do you have meals/
drinks for diabetics?

¿Tienen comidas/bebidas para diabéticos?
*teeyenen komeedas/bebeedas para
deeya beteekos*

Do you have
vegetarian meals?

¿Tienen comidas vegetarianas?
teeyenen komeedas bekhetareeyanas

For the children

Do you have children's
portions?

¿Hacen porciones para niños?
athen portheeyones para neeños

Could we have a
child's seat, please?

¿Podrían ponernos una silla para niños?
*podreeyan ponernos oona seel-ya
para neeños*

Where can I feed/
change the baby?

**¿Dónde puedo darle de comer/cambiar
al niño?** *dondeh pwedo darleh deh
komer/kambeeyar al neeño*

FAST FOOD/CAFÉ

Something to drink

I'd like (a) …	**Quiero …** *keeyero*
beer	**una cerveza** *oona therbetha*
tea/coffee/chocolate	**un té/un café/un chocolate** *oon teh/oon kafeh/oon chokolateh*
black/with milk	**solo/con leche** *solo/kon lecheh*
fruit juice/mineral water	**un zumo de fruta/un agua mineral** *oon thoomo deh froota/oon agwa meeneral*
red/white wine	**un vino tinto/blanco** *oon beeno teento/blanko*

YOU MAY HEAR

¿Qué va a tomar?	What would you like?
No tenemos …	We've run out of …
¿Algo más?	Anything else?

And to eat

I'd like two of those.	**Quiero dos de esos.** *keeyero dos deh esos*
burger/omelet	**una hamburguesa/una tortilla francesa** *oona amboorgesa/oona torteel-ya franthesa*
fries [chips]/sandwich	**patatas fritas/un bocadillo** *patatas freetas/oon bokadeel-yo*
cake *(small/large)*	**un dulce/una tarta** *oon dooltheh/oona tarta*
A … ice cream, please.	**Un helado de …, por favor.** *oon elado deh … por fabor*
chocolate/strawberry/vanilla	**chocolate/fresa/vainilla** *chokolateh/fresa/bayneel-ya*
A … portion, please.	**Una porción …, por favor.** *oona portheeyon … por fabor*
small/medium/large	**pequeña/mediana/grande** *pekeña/medeeyana/grandeh*
It's to go [take away].	**Para llevar.** *para l-yebar*
That's all, thanks.	**Eso es todo, gracias.** *eso es todo, gratheeyas*

IN A CAFÉ

Dos cafés, por favor. *dos kafehs por fabor*
(Two coffees, please.)
¿Algo más? *algo mas (Anything else?)*
Eso es todo. Gracias. *eso es todo gratheeyas*
(That's all, thanks.)

COMPLAINTS

I have no knife/fork/spoon.	**No tengo cuchillo/tenedor/cuchara.** *no tengo koocheel-yo/tenedor/koochara*
There must be some mistake.	**Debe de haber un error.** *debeh deh aber oon error*
That's not what I ordered.	**Eso no es lo que pedí.** *eso no es lo keh pedee*
I asked for …	**Pedí …** *pedee*
I can't eat this.	**No puedo comerme esto.** *no pwedo komermeh esto*
The meat is …	**La carne está …** *la karneh esta*
overdone	**demasiado hecha** *demaseeyado echa*
underdone	**cruda** *krooda*
too tough	**demasiado dura** *demaseeyado doora*
This is too …	**Esto está demasiado …** *esto esta demaseeyado*
The food is cold.	**La comida está fría.** *la komeeda esta freeya*
This isn't fresh.	**Esto no está fresco.** *esto no esta fresko*
How much longer will our food be?	**¿Cuánto más tardará la comida?** *kwanto mas tardara la komeeda*
We can't wait any longer. We're leaving.	**No podemos esperar más. Nos vamos.** *no podemos esperar mas. nos bamos*
Have you forgotten our drinks?	**¿Se le han olvidado las bebidas?** *seh leh an olbeedado las bebeedas*
This isn't clean.	**Esto no está limpio.** *esto no esta leempeeyo*
I'd like to speak to the head waiter/manager.	**Quiero hablar con el metre/encargado.** *keeyero ablar kon el metreh/enkargado*

Paying

Tipping: Service is generally included in the bill, but if you are happy with the service, a personal tip of €1 per person up to 10% for the waiter is appropriate and appreciated.

The bill, please.	**La cuenta, por favor.** *la kwenta por fabor*
We'd like to pay separately.	**Queremos pagar por separado.** *keremos pagar por separado*
It's all together, please.	**Póngalo todo junto, por favor.** *pongalo todo khoonto por fabor*
I think there's a mistake in this bill.	**Creo que hay un error en esta cuenta.** *kreyo keh eye oon error en esta kwenta*
What is this amount for?	**¿De qué es esta cantidad?** *deh keh es esta kanteedath*
I didn't have that. I had …	**Yo no tomé eso. Yo tomé …** *yo no tomeh eso. yo tomeh*
Is service included?	**¿Está el servicio incluido?** *esta el serbeetheeyo eenklooweedo*
Can I pay with this credit card?	**¿Puedo pagar con esta tarjeta de crédito?** *pwedo pagar kon esta tarkheta deh kredeeto*
Could I have a VAT receipt?	**¿Podría darme un recibo?** *podreeya darmeh oon retheebopor*
Can I have an itemized bill?	**¿Podría darme una cuenta detallada?** *odreeya darmeh oona kwenta detal-yada*
That was a very good meal.	**La comida estuvo muy buena.** *la komeeda estoobo mwee bwena*

Course by course

Breakfast

I'd like …	**Quiero …** *keeyero*
bread	**pan** *pan*
butter	**mantequilla** *mantekeel-ya*

fried eggs	**huevos fritos** _weboss freetoss_
scrambled eggs	**huevos revueltos** _weboss rebweltoss_
fruit juice	**un zumo de fruta**
	oon thoomo deh froota
jam	**mermelada** _mermelada_
milk	**leche** _lecheh_
roll	**panecillo** _penetheel-yo_

Appetizers/Starters

Croquetas _kroketass_
Croquettes made with ham, fish, egg or a wide variety of other fillings.

Ensaladilla rusa _ensaladeel-ya rroossa_
Potatoes with peas, tuna, boiled eggs and olives mixed with mayonnaise.

Champiñones al ajillo _champeeñones ahl akheel-yo_
Mushrooms fried in olive oil with garlic.

Tapas _tapass_
A huge variety of snacks served in cafés and tapa bars, ranging from meat balls, cheese, smoked ham, mushrooms, fried fish plus sauces and exotic-looking specialties of the house. **Una tapa** is a mouthful, **una ración** half a plateful, and **una porción** a generous amount.

aceitunas (rellenas)	_athetoonass (rel-yenass)_	(stuffed) olives
albóndigas	_albondee-ass_	spiced meatballs
almejas	_almekhass_	clams
calamares	_kalamaress_	squid
callos	_kal-yoss_	tripe (in hot paprika sauce)
caracoles	_karakoless_	snails
chorizo	_choreetho_	spicy sausage
gambas	_gambass_	prawns (shrimps)
jamón	_khamon_	ham
mejillones	_mekheel-yoness_	mussels
pimientos	_peemyentoss_	peppers
pinchos	_peenchoss_	grilled skewered meat

IN A RESTAURANT

¡Camarero! kama*re*ro (Waiter!)
Sí, señora. see sen*yoh*ra (Yes, m'am.)
El menú, por favor. el me*noo* por fa*bor* (The menu, please.)
Sí, cómo no. see *ko*mo no (Sure.)

Soups

caldo gallego	*kal*do gal-*ye*go	meat and vegetable broth
consomé al jerez	konso*meh* al khe*reth*	chicken broth with sherry
sopa de ajo	*so*pa deh *a*kho	garlic soup
sopa de fideos	*so*pa deh fee*dey*oss	noodle soup
sopa de mariscos	*so*pa deh ma*ree*skoss	seafood soup
sopa de verduras	*so*pa deh ber*doo*rass	vegetable soup

Ajo blanco *a*kho *blan*ko
Cold garlic and almond soup garnished with grapes (*Andalucia*).

Gazpacho gath*pa*cho
A cold tomato soup with cucumber, green pepper, bread, onion, and garlic.

Sopa castellana sopa kasteel-*ya*na
Baked garlic soup with chunks of ham and a poached egg,

Sopa de cocido *so*pa deh ko*thee*do
Broth, with beef, ham, sausage, chickpeas, cabbage, turnip, onion, and potatoes.

Egg dishes

Huevos a la flamenca *we*boss a la fla*men*ka
Eggs baked with tomato, onion and diced ham..

Huevos al nido *we*boss al *nee*do
"Eggs in the nest," egg yolks set in soft rolls, fried and covered in egg white.

Huevos rellenos *we*boss rrel-*ye*nos
Boiled eggs filled with tuna fish and dressed with mayonnaise.

Tortilla tor*tee*l-ya
Round Spanish omelet; popular varieties include: **~ de patatas** (potato with onions), **~ de jamón** (ham), **~ paisana** (potatoes, peas, prawns or ham), **~ de queso** (cheese), **~ de setas** (mushroom).

Fish and seafood

atún	_atoon_	tuna
bacalao	_bakalao_	cod
boquerones	_bokeroness_	herring
caballa	_kabal-ya_	mackerel
chipirones	_cheepeeroness_	baby squid
langosta	_langosta_	lobster
mero	_mero_	sea bass
pez espada	_peth espada_	swordfish
pulpo	_poolpo_	octopus
trucha	_troocha_	trout

Bacalao a la catalana _bakalao a la katalana_
Salt cod in ratatouille sauce, with onions, eggplant, zucchini [courgettes], tomatoes, and pepper.

Calamares a la romana _kalamaress al la rromana_
Squid rings deep fried in batter.

Pulpo a la gallega _poolpo a la gal-yega_
Octopus dressed with olive oil and paprika.

Lenguado a la vasca _lengwado a la baska_
Baked sole with sliced potatoes in a mushroom, red pepper, and tomato sauce.

Trucha a la navarra _troocha a la nabarra_
Grilled trout stuffed with ham.

Paella

Basically, paella is made of saffron rice garnished with meat, fish, seafood and/or vegetables. Here are four of the most popular ways of preparing paella.

Paella de verduras _pa-el-ya de berdoorass_
Artichokes, peas, broad beans, cauliflower, garlic, peppers, tomato.

Paella de marisco _pa-el-ya de mareesko_
Fish and seafood only.

Paella valenciana _pa-el-ya balenthyana_
Chicken, shrimp, mussels, prawn, squid, peas, tomato, chili pepper, garlic.

Paella zamorana _pa-el-ya thamorana_
Ham, pork loin, pig's feet, chili pepper.

Meat

carne de buey	*karneh deh bwehee*	beef
carne de cerdo	*karneh deh therdo*	pork
carne de cordero	*karneh deh kordero*	lamb
carne de ternera	*karneh deh ternera*	veal
chuletas	*chooletass*	chops
conejo	*konekho*	rabbit
filete	*feeleteh*	steak
hígado	*eegado*	liver
jamón	*khamon*	ham
pato	*pato*	duck
pavo	*pavo*	turkey
pollo	*pol-yo*	chicken
riñones	*reeñoness*	kidneys
salchichas	*salcheechass*	sausages
tocino	*totheeno*	bacon

Specialties

Asado de cordero *assado deh kordero*
Roast lamb with garlic and wine.

Cochinillo asado *kocheeneel-yo assado*
Crispy roasted suckling pig.

Cocido madrileño *kotheedo madreeleño*
Hotpot, stew.

Empanada gallega *empanada gal-yega*
Pork and onion pie.

Estofado de ternera *estofado deh ternera*
Veal stew with wine, carrots, onions, and potatoes.

Lomo de cerdo al jerez *lomo deh therdo al khereth*
Roast loin of pork with sherry.

Pollo en pepitoria *pol-yo en pepeetoreeya*
Chicken in egg and almond sauce.

Riñones al jerez *rreeñoness al khereth*
Lamb kidneys in an onion and sherry sauce.

Vegetables

arroz	*ar<u>roth</u>*	rice
berenjena	*bere<u>kh</u>ena*	eggplant [aubergine]
cebolla	*the<u>bol</u>-ya*	onion
champiñones	*champee<u>ño</u>ness*	button mushrooms
guisantes	*qee<u>ss</u>antes*	peas
judías verdes	*khoo<u>dee</u>ass <u>ver</u>dess*	green beans
lechuga	*le<u>choo</u>ga*	lettuce
patatas	*pa<u>ta</u>tas*	potatoes
pimientos morrones	*peem<u>yen</u>tos mo<u>rro</u>ness*	sweet red peppers
repollo	*re<u>pol</u>-yo*	cabbage
setas	*<u>se</u>tass*	mushrooms
zanahorias	*thana-<u>or</u>yass*	carrots

Ensalada *ensa<u>la</u>da*
Salad; typical varieties to look out for: **~ de atún** (tuna), **~ de lechuga** (green); **~ de pepino** (cucumber), **~ del tiempo** (seasonal), **~ valenciana** (with green peppers, lettuce, and oranges).

Lentejas estofadas *len<u>te</u>khass esto<u>fa</u>dass*
Green lentils with onions, tomatoes, carrots, and garlic.

Pisto *<u>pees</u>to*
A stew of green peppers, onions, tomatoes, and zucchini [courgettes]; you might also see it referred to as **frito de verduras**.

Fruit

cerezas	*the<u>re</u>thass*	cherries
ciruelas	*thee<u>rwe</u>lass*	plums
frambuesas	*fram<u>bwe</u>sass*	raspberries
fresas	*<u>fre</u>sass*	strawberries
manzana	*man<u>tha</u>na*	apple
melocotón	*meloko<u>ton</u>*	peach
naranja	*na<u>ran</u>kha*	orange
plátano	*<u>pla</u>tano*	banana
pomelo	*po<u>me</u>lo*	grapefruit
uvas	*<u>oo</u>vass*	grapes

Cheese

Burgos _boorgos_
A soft, creamy cheese named after the province from which it originates.

Cabrales _kabrales_
A tangy, veined goat cheese; its flavor varies, depending upon the mountain region in which it was produced.

Manchego _manchego_
Produced from ewe's milk, this hard cheese from La Mancha can vary from milky white to golden yellow. The best is said to come from Ciudad Real.

Perilla _pereel-ya_
A firm, bland cheese made from cow's milk; sometimes known as **teta**.

Roncal _rronkal_
A sharp ewe's milk cheese from northern Spain; hand-pressed, salted and smoked with leathery rind.

blue	**tipo roquefort**	mild		**suave** _swabeh_
	teepo rrokefort	ripe		**curado** _kurado_
cream	**cremoso** _kremosso_	soft		**blando** _blando_
hard	**duro** _dooro_	strong		**fuerte** _fwerteh_

Dessert

bizcocho	_beethkocho_	sponge cake
brazo de gitano	_bratho deh geetano_	rum cream roll
canutillos	_kanooteel-yos_	custard horns with cinnamon
crema catalana	_krema katalana_	caramel pudding
flan	_flan_	crème caramel
fritos	_freetos_	fritters
galletas	_gal-yetas_	cookies [biscuits]
mantecado	_mantekado_	rich almond ice cream
pastel de queso	_pastel deh keso_	cheesecake
tarta de manzana	_tarta deh manthana_	apple tart
tortitas	_torteetas_	waffles

Helado _elado_
Ice cream; popular flavors include: ~ **de chocolate** (chocolate), ~ **de fresa** (strawberry), **de limón** (lemon), ~ **de moka** (mocha), ~ **de vainilla** (vanilla).

DRINKS

Aperitifs

For most Spaniards, a before-dinner drink of vermouth or sherry is as important as our cocktail or highball. Vermouth (**vermut**) is rarely drunk neat but usually on the rocks or with seltzer water. Some Spaniards content themselves with a glass of local wine. You'll probably be given a dish of olives or nuts to nibble on. Or in a bar specializing in tapas, you can order various snacks.

Sherry (**jerez** *khereth*) is Spain's most renowned drink. It has alcohol or brandy added to "fortify" it during the fermentation process. Sherry was the first fortified wine to become popular in England – "sherry" derives from the English spelling of the town **Jerez**, where the wine originated.

Major sherry producers include Lustau, Osborne, Pedro Domecq, Antonio Barbadillo, Gonzalez Byass, Bobadilla, House of Sandeman, Valdespino, John Harvey & Sons.

Sherry can be divided into two groups:

Fino *feeno*

These are the pale, dry sherries that make good aperitifs. The Spaniards themselves are especially fond of **amontillado** and **manzanilla**. Some of the best **finos** are Tío Pepe and La Ina.

Oloroso *olorosso*

These are the heavier, darker sherries that are sweetened before being bottled. They're fine after-dinner drinks. One exception is **amoroso** which is medium dry. Brown and cream sherries are full-bodied and slightly less fragrant than **finos**.

Beer

Spanish beer, generally served cool, is good and relatively inexpensive. Try **Águila especial** or **San Miguel especial**.

A beer, please.	**Una cerveza, por favor.** *oona therbetha por fabor*
light beer	**cerveza rubia** *therbetha roobya*
dark beer	**cerveza negra** *therbetha negra*
foreign beer	**cerveza extranjera** *therbetha ekstrankhera*
small/large beer	**cerveza pequeña/grande** *therbetha pekeña/grandeh*

Wine

Spain has the largest area under vine in the world and is the third largest producer and exporter.

Spain's best wine comes from **Rioja**, a region of Old Castile of which **Logroño** is the center. Wine makers there add **garantía de origen** to wine they feel is of above average quality.

The **Penedés** region near Barcelona is a major source of the world's best-selling white sparkling wine, **cava**.

Traditionally, white wine goes well with fish, fowl and light meats, while dark meats call for a red wine. A good rosé or dry sparkling **Cava** goes well with almost anything.

Ask for the patron's own wine "**el vino de la casa**"; you should receive a good wine, corresponding to the quality of the establishment.

I want a bottle of white/red wine.	**Quiero una botella de vino blanco/tinto.** *keeyero oona botel-ya deh beeno blanko/teento*
a carafe	**una garrafa** *oona garrafa*
a half bottle	**media botella** *medya botel-ya*
a glass	**un vaso** *oon basso*
a small glass	**un chato** *oon chato*
a liter	**un litro** *oon leetro*
a jar	**una jarra** *oona kharra*

añejo mature	**joven** young
blanco white	**liviano** light
bodegas cellar	**moscatel** sweet dessert wine
cava white, sparkling wine	**muy seco** very dry
de cuerpo full-bodied	**reserva** aged over 3 years
DO (Denominación de Origen) regulated quality	**rosado** rosé
	seco dry
DOCa superior wine (Rioja only)	**tinto** red
dulce sweet	**vino de calidad** quality wine
embotellado en bottled in	**vino de cosecha** vintage wine
espumoso sparkling	**vino de crianza** aged in oak
gran reserva aged 3 years in a barrel then 3 years in the bottle (exceptional years only)	barrels for minimum of 6 months

Wine regions

Aragón Campo de Borja, Calatayud, Cariñena, Navarra, Rioja (Alta, Alavesa, Baja), Somotano

País Vasco Chacolí de Guetaria, Rioja Alavesa

Castilla y León Bierzo, Cigales, Ribera del Duero, Rueda, Toro

Cataluña Alella, Ampurdán-Costa Brava, Conca de Barberà, Costers del Segre, Penedès (center of the Cava sparkling wine region), Priorato, Tarragona, Terra Alta

Galicia Rías Baixas, Ribeiro, Valdeorras

Central Spain Alicante, Almansa, Bullas, Jumilla, La Mancha, Levante, Méntrida, Utiel-Requena, Valdepeñas, Valencia, Vinos de Madrid, Yecla

Southern Spain Condado de Huelva, Jerez, Málaga, Manzanilla-Sanlúcar de Barrameda, Montilla-Moriles

Islands Binissalem (Balearic), Tacoronte-Acentejo (Canaries)

Spirits and liqueurs

You'll recognize: **ginebra** (gin), **ron** (rum), **oporto** (port wine), **vermut**, **vodka**, and **whisky**.

double (a double shot)	**doble**	_dobleh_
straight/neat	**solo**	_solo_
on the rocks	**con hielo**	_kon yelo_
with soda/tonic	**con soda/tónica**	_kon soda/toneeka_

Sangría _sangreea_

wine punch/cup made with red wine, fruit juice, brandy, slices of fruit, diluted with soda and ice; ideal for hot weather

Non-alcoholic drinks

I'd like a cup of coffee.	**Quiero una taza de café.**	
	keeyero oona tatha deh kafeh	
(hot) chocolate	**un chocolate (caliente)**	
	oon chokolateh (kaliyenteh)	
iced fruit juice	**un granizado**	_oon graneethado_
lemonade	**una limonada**	_oona leemonada_
milk	**leche**	_lecheh_
milk shake	**un batido**	_oon bateedo_
orangeade	**una naranjada**	_oona narankhada_
(iced/mineral) water	**agua (helada/mineral)**	_agwa (elada/meeneral)_

MENU READER

This Menu Reader is an alphabetical glossary of terms that you may find in a menu. Certain traditional dishes are cross-referenced to the relevant page in the *Course by course* section, where they are described in more detail.

adobado(-a)	*adobado(-a)*	marinated
ahumado(-a)	*ahoomado*	smoked
a la brasa	*a la brasa*	braised
al grill	*al greel*	grilled
al horno	*al orno*	baked
al vapor	*al bapor*	steamed
asado(-a)	*asado*	roasted
bien hecho(-a)	*beeyen echo*	well-done
con especias	*kon espetheeyas*	spicy
con nata	*kon nata*	creamed
cortado en taquitos	*kortado en takeetos*	diced
dorado(-a) al horno	*dorado(-a) al orno*	oven-browned
empanado(-a)	*empanado(-a)*	breaded
escaldado(-a)	*eskaldado(-a)*	poached
frito(-a)	*freeto(-a)*	fried
guisado(-a)	*geesado(-a)*	stewed
hervido(-a)	*erbeedo*	boiled
medio hecho(-a)	*medeeyo echo*	medium
muy poco hecho(-a)	*mwee poko echo(-a)*	rare
poco hecho(-a)	*poko echo*	medium rare
refrito(-a)	*refreeto(-a)*	sautéed
relleno(-a)	*rel-yeno(-a)*	stuffed

A

a la parrilla grilled/broiled
a la romana deep-fried
a punto medium (done)
abocado sherry made from sweet and dry wine
acedera sorrel

aceitunas (rellenas) (stuffed) olives
achicoria chicory
agua water; ~ **caliente** hot water; ~ **helada** iced water; ~ **mineral** mineral water
aguacate avocado
aguardiente spirits (eau-de-vie)
ahumado smoked

ajo garlic; **~ blanco** garlic soup

ajoaceite garlic mayonnaise

al adobo marinated

al ajillo in garlic and oil

al horno baked

albahaca basil

albaricoques apricots

albóndigas spiced meatballs

alcachofas artichokes

alcaparra caper

alioli garlic mayonnaise

aliñado seasoned

almejas clams; **~ a la marinera** cooked in hot, pimento sauce

almendra almond; **~ garrapiñada** sugared

almuerzo lunch

almíbar syrup

alubia bean

amontillado medium-dry sherry with nutty taste

anchoas anchovies

añejo mature

anguila ahumada smoked eel

angula baby eel

Angélica Basque herb liqueur

anisado aniseed-based soft drink

anticucho beef heart grilled on skewer with green peppers

anís anisette

aperitivos aperitifs

apio celery

arándanos blueberries

arenque (ahumado) (smoked) herring

arepa pancake made of corn (maize)

arroz rice; **~ a la cubana** boiled rice served with tomato sauce and a fried egg; **~ a la valenciana** with vegetables, chicken, shellfish; **~ blanco** boiled, steamed; **~ negro** with seafood and squid ink; **~ primavera** with spring vegetables; **~ con costra** with pork meatballs; **~ con leche** rice pudding

asado roast

asturias (queso de ...) strong, fermented cheese

atún tuna

avellanas hazelnuts

aves poultry

azafrán saffron

azúcar sugar

B

bacalao cod

banderillas gherkins, chile peppers and olives on a skewer

batata sweet potato, yam

batido milk shake

bebidas drinks

bebidas sin alcohol non-alcoholic drinks

becada woodcock

berberecho cockle

berenjena eggplant/aubergine

berraza parsnip

berro cress

berza cabbage

besugo (sea) bream

bien hecho well-done

biftec beef steak

bizcocho sponge cake; **~ borracho** steeped in rum and syrup

bizcotela glazed cookie/biscuit

blanco white

blando soft; medium

Bobadilla Gran Reserva wine-distilled brandy

bocadillo sandwich

bocadillo de jamón ham sandwich

bollos cake

bonito tuna

boquerones kind of anchovy

botella bottle

brevas blue figs

(en) brocheta (on a) skewer

budín blancmange, custard

buey ox

burgos (queso de ...) soft, creamy cheese

buñuelitos small fritters

C

caballa mackerel

cabra goat

cabrales (queso de ...) tangy goat cheese

cabrito kid

cacahuetes peanuts

café coffee

calabacín zucchini [courgette]

calabaza pumpkin

calamares squid; **~ a la romana** fried in batter

caldereta de cabrito kid stew

caldillo de congrio conger-eel soup with tomatoes and potatoes

caldo consommé

caldo gallego meat and vegetable broth

caliente hot

Calisay quinine-flavored liqueur

callos tripe; **~ a la madrileña** tripe in piquant sauce with spicy pork sausage and tomatoes

camarón shrimp

canela cinnamon

cangrejo (de mar/de río) crab/crayfish

cantarela chanterelle mushroom

capón capon

caracoles snails

caramelos candy; sweets

Carlos I wine-distilled brandy

carne meat

carne a la parrilla charcoal-grilled steak

carne de buey beef

carne de cangrejo crabmeat

carne de cerdo pork

carne de cordero lamb

carne de ternera veal

carne molida chopped/minced beef

carne picada chopped/minced meat

carnero mutton

carta menu; **a la ~** a la carte

casero homemade

castanola sea perch

castañas chestnuts

catalana spicy pork sausages

caza game

(a la) cazadora with mushrooms, spring onions, herbs in wine

Cazalla aniseed liqueur

cazuela de cordero lamb stew with vegetables

cebollas onions
cebolleta spring onion
cebollinos chives
cebrero (queso de ...) blue-veined cheese
cena dinner, supper
centolla spider-crab, served cold
cerdo pork
cereales cereal
cerezas cherries
cerveza beer
chalote shallot
champiñones button mushrooms
chancho adobado pork braised with sweet potatoes, orange and lemon juice
chanfaina goat's liver and kidney stew, served in a thick sauce
chanquete herring/whitebait
chato a small glass
chile chili pepper
chilindrón sauce of tomatoes, peppers, garlic, ham and wine *(Pyr.)*
chimichurri hot parsley sauce
Chinchón aniseed liqueur
chipirones baby squid
chirivías parsnips
chocolate (caliente) (hot) chocolate
chopa type of sea bream
chorizo spicy sausage made of pork, garlic and paprika
chuletas chops
chupe de mariscos scallops served with creamy sauce and gratinéed with cheese
churro sugared tubular fritter
cigalas sea crayfish [Dublin Bay prawns]

cincho (queso de ...) hard sheep-milk cheese
ciruelas plums; **~ pasas** prunes
clavo clove
cochifrito de cordero highly seasoned stew of lamb or kid
cochinillo asado crispy roasted Castilian suckling pig
cocido boiled; beef stew with ham, fowl, chickpeas, and potatoes
cocido al vapor steamed
coco coconut
codorniz quail
cohombrillos pickles/gherkins
cola de mono blend of coffee, milk, rum, and pisco
coles de bruselas Brussels sprouts
coliflor cauliflower
comida meal
comino caraway
compota stewed fruit
con hielo on the rocks
con leche with milk
con limón with lemon
condimentos herbs
coñac brandy
conejo rabbit; **~ al ajillo** rabbit with garlic; **~ de monte** wild rabbit
confitura jam
congrio conger eel
consomé al jerez chicken broth with sherry
copa nuria egg yolk and egg white, whipped and served with jam
corazonada heart stewed in sauce
corazón heart
cordero lamb

Cordoníu brand of Catalonian sparkling wine

cortadillo small pancake with lemon

corto strong coffee

corzo deer

costilla chop

crema cream; **~ batida** whipped cream; **~ catalana** caramel pudding; **~ española** dessert of milk, eggs, and fruit jelly; **~ nieve** with beaten egg yolk, sugar, rum

cremoso cream

criadillas sweetbreads

(a la) criolla with green peppers, spices and tomatoes

croqueta fish or meat cake

crudo raw

Cuarenta y Tres egg liqueur

Cuba libre rum coke

cubierto cover charge

cuenta bill, check

curanto dish of seafood, vegetables and suckling pig

D

damasco variety of apricot

dátiles dates

de cordero lamb's

de cuerpo full-bodied

de lechuga green

de ternera calf's

del tiempo in season

desayuno breakfast

descafeinado decaffeinated

doble double (a double shot)

dulce dessert wine; sweet

dulce de naranja marmelade

durazno peach

duro hard *(egg)*

E

edulcorante sweetener

embuchado stuffed with meat

embutido spicy sausage

empanada pie or tart with meat or fish filling; **~ de horno** filled with minced meat; **~ gallega** tenderloin of pork, onions and chili peppers in a pie

empanadillas small savory pastries stuffed with meat or fish

empanado breaded

emperador swordfish

en dulce boiled

en escabeche marinated

en salazón cured

en salsa braised in casserole

en su jugo pot roasted

enchilada tortilla stuffed and served with vegetable garnish and sauce

encurtido pickled

endibia endive

eneldo dill

ensalada salad; **~ rusa** diced cold vegetables with mayonnaise

entremeses (variados) (assorted) appetizers

escabeche de gallina chicken marinated in vinegar and bay leaves

escarola escarole

espaguetis spaghetti

espalda shoulder

(a la) española with tomatoes

especialidades de la casa specialties of the house

especialidades locales local specialties

especias spices

espinacas spinach

espumoso sparkling

espárragos (puntas de) asparagus (tips)

esqueixado *(Cat.)* mixed fish salad

(al) estilo de in the style of

estofado braised; stewed

estragón tarragon

F

fabada (asturiana) stew of pork, beans, bacon and sausage

faisán pheasant

fiambres cold cuts

fideo thin noodle

filete steak; **~ de lenguado empanado** breaded fillet of sole; **~ de lomo** fillet steak (tenderloin); **~ de res** beef steak

fino pale, dry sherry

(a la) flamenca with onions, peas, green peppers, tomatoes and spiced sausage

flan caramel pudding

frambuesas raspberries

(a la) francesa sautéed in butter

fresas strawberries

fresco fresh, chilled

fresón large strawberry

fricandó thin slice of meat rolled in bacon and braised

frijoles beans; **~ refritos** fried mashed beans

frito fried; **~ de patata** deep-fried potato croquette

fritos fritters

fritura mixta meat, fish or vegetables deep-fried in batter

fruta fruit; **~ escarchada** candied fruit

frío cold

fuerte strong

Fundador wine-distilled brandy

G

galletas cookies [biscuits]; **~ de nata** cream cookies; **~ saladas** crackers

gallina hen

gallo cockerel

gambas (grandes) shrimp [prawns]; **~ a la plancha** grilled; **~ al ajillo** with garlic

ganso goose

garbanzos chickpeas

garrafa carafe

gaseosa carbonated/fizzy

gazpacho cold tomato soup

ginebra gin; **~ con limón** gin-fizz; **~ con tónica** gin and tonic

(a la) gitanilla with garlic

gordo fatty, rich

granadas pomegranates

granadina pomegranate syrup mixed with wine or brandy

granizados iced drinks

gratinado gratinéed

grelos turnip greens

grosellas espinosas gooseberries

grosellas negras blackcurrants

grosellas rojas redcurrants

guacamole spicy avocado salad

guarnición garnish, trimming
guayaba guava *(fruit)*
guinda sour cherry
guindilla chili pepper
guisado stewed
guisantes peas

H

habas broad beans
habichuela verde French/green beans
hamburguesa hamburger
hayaca central cornmeal pancake, usually with minced-meat filling
helado ice cream
hervido boiled; poached
hielo ice
hierbas herbs; **~ finas** mixture of herbs
higaditos de pollo chicken livers
hígado liver
higos figs
hinojo fennel
hoja de laurel bay leaf
hongos fungi
horchata de almendra/chufa ground almond drink
(al) horno baked
hueso bone
huevos eggs; **~ a la española** stuffed with tomatoes and served with cheese sauce; **~ a la flamenca** baked with tomato, onion and diced ham; **~ al nido** "eggs in the nest"; **~ al trote** with tuna;
~ cocidos boiled; **~ duros** hard-boiled eggs; **~ escalfados a la**

española poached egg on onions, tomatoes, peppers and zucchini;
~ fritos fried eggs; **~ revueltos** scrambled eggs
humita boiled corn with tomatoes, green peppers, onions, and cheese

J

jabalí wild boar
jalea jelly
jamón ham; **~ en dulce** boiled and served cold; **~ y huevos** ham and eggs
(a la) jardinera with carrots, peas, and other vegetables
jengibre ginger
jerez sherry
judías blancas white beans
judías verdes green beans
jugo fresh juice; gravy, meat juice; **~ de fruta** fruit juice
jurel kind of mackerel *(fish)*

L

lacón shoulder of pork
lampreas lampreys
langosta lobster; **~ con pollo** with chicken
langostinos shrimp [prawns]
lavanco wild duck
leche milk
lechón suckling pig
lechuga lettuce
legumbres pulses
lengua tongue
lenguado sole; **~ a la vasca** baked with potatoes and vegetables
lentejas lentils

licor liqueur
liebre hare; **~ estofada** jugged
lima lime
limonada lemonade
limón lemon
lista de platos menu
lista de vinos wine list
litro a liter
liviano light
lobarro type of bass
lombarda red cabbage
lomo loin; **~ de cerdo al jerez** pork loin
loncha slice of meat
longaniza long, highly seasoned sausage
lubina bass

M

macedonia de frutas mixed fruit salad
(a la) madrileña with chorizo sausage, tomatoes and paprika
magras al estilo de Aragón cured ham in tomato sauce
Mahón (queso de ...) type of goat cheese
(a la) mallorquina highly seasoned (fish and shellfish)
maíz sweet corn
manchego (queso de ...) ewe's milk cheese
mandarina tangerine
mantecado rich almond ice cream
mantequilla butter
manzana apple

manzanilla dry, pale sherry
maní peanut
marinera fish and seafood only
(a la) marinera with mussels, onions, tomatoes, herbs, and wine
mariscos seafood
matambre rolled beef stuffed with vegetables
mazapán marzipan
media botella half bottle
medio pollo asado half a roasted chicken
mejillones mussels
melaza treacle, molasses
melocotón peach; **~ en almíbar** in syrup
melón melon
membrillo quince paste
menestra green vegetable soup; **~ de pollo** casserole of chicken and vegetables
menta mint
menudillos giblets
merengue meringue
merienda afternoon snack
merluza hake
mermelada jam; **~ amarga de naranjas** marmalade
mero sea bass
miel honey
(a la) milanese with cheese, generally baked
minuta menu
mojo picón piquant red sauce *(Can.)*
mojo verde green herb sauce served with fish *(Cat.)*

mole poblano chicken served with sauce of chili peppers, spices and chocolate

mollejas sweetbreads

moras mulberries

morcilla blood sausage *(black pudding)*

morilla morel mushroom

moros y cristianos rice and black beans with diced ham, garlic, green peppers and herbs

mostaza mustard

mújol mullet *(fish)*

muslo de pollo chicken leg

muy hecho well-done

muy seco very dry

N

nabo turnip

naranja orange

naranjada orangeade

nata cream; ~ **batida** whipped

natillas custard

níspola medlar *(fruit)*

nopalito young cactus leaf served with salad dressing

nueces walnuts

nueces variadas assorted nuts

nuez moscada nutmeg

O

olla stew; ~ **gitana** vegetable stew; ~ **podrida** stew made of vegetables, meat, fowl and ham

oloroso dark sherry

oporto port

ostras oysters

oveja ewe

P

pa amb tomàquet bread with tomato and salt *(Cat.)*

pabellón criollo beef in tomato sauce, garnished with beans, rice and bananas

paella paella

paletilla shank

palitos skewered appetizer ~ **de queso** cheese sticks/straws

palmito palm heart

palta avocado

pan bread; ~ **de pueblo** plain white bread

panecillos rolls

papas potatoes; ~ **a la huancaína** with cheese and green peppers; ~ **arrugadas** new potatoes baked and rolled in rock salt *(Can.)*

parrillada grill; ~ **mixta** mixed

pasado done, cooked; ~ **por agua** soft *(egg)*

pasas raisins

pastas pastry; pasta

pastel cake; ~ **de choclo** corn [maize] with minced beef, chicken, raisins, and olives; ~ **de queso** cheesecake

pasteles cakes; pastries

patatas potatoes; ~ **(a la) leonesa** potatoes with onions; ~ **fritas** French fries [chips]; ~ **nuevas** new potatoes

pato duck/duckling

paté pâté

pavo turkey

pechuga de pollo breast of chicken
pepinillos pickles/gherkins
pepino cucumber
(en) pepitoria stewed with onions, green peppers and tomatoes
pera pear
perca perch *(fish)*
percebes goose barnacles *(seafood)*
perdiz partridge; **~ en escabeche** cooked in oil with vinegar, onions, parsley, carrots and green pepper; served cold; **~ estofada** served in a white-wine sauce
perejil parsley
perifollo chervil
perilla (queso de ...) firm cheese
pescadilla whiting *(fish)*
pescado fish **~ frito** fried fish
pez espada swordfish
picadillo minced meat, hash
picado minced
picante sharp, spicy, highly seasoned
picatoste deep-fried slice of bread
pichón pigeon
pierna leg
pimentón paprika
pimienta pepper
pimientos a la riojana sweet peppers stuffed with minced meat
pimientos morrones sweet red peppers
piña pineapple
pincho moruno grilled meat on a skewer

pintada guinea fowl
pisco grape brandy
pisto green pepper stew
(a la) plancha grilled on a griddle
plato plate, dish, portion; **~ del día** dish of the day
platos fríos cold dishes
platos típicos specialties
plátano banana
poco hecho rare
pollito spring chicken
pollo chicken; **~ a la brasa** grilled; **~ asado** roast; **~ pibil** simmered in fruit juice and spices
polvorón almond cookie [biscuit]
pomelo grapefruit
ponche crema eggnog liquor
porción small helping of tapas
postre dessert
potaje vegetable soup
puchero stew
puerros leeks
pulpitos baby octopus
pulpo octopus
punto de nieve dessert of whipped cream with beaten egg whites
puré purée; **~ de patatas** mashed potatoes

Q

queso cheese
quisquillas common shrimps

R

rábano radish; **~ picante** horseradish
rabo de buey oxtail

ración large helping
raja slice, portion
rallado grated
rape monkfish
raya ray, skate
rebanada slice
rebozado breaded, fried in batter
recomendamos … we recommend …
refrescos cold drinks
regular medium
rehogada sautéed
relleno stuffed
remolacha beet [beetroot]
repollo cabbage
requesón (queso de …) cottage cheese [fresh-curd cheese]
riñones kidneys; **~ al jerez** braised in sherry
róbalo haddock
rodaballo turbot
(a la) romana dipped in batter and fried
romero rosemary
romesco sauce of nuts, chili, tomatoes, garlic, and breadcrumbs *(Cat.)*
ron rum
roncal (queso de …) sharp ewe's milk cheese
ropa vieja cooked, leftover meat and vegetables, covered with tomatoes and green peppers
rosado rosé
rosbif roast beef
rosquilla doughnut
rubio red mullet
ruibarbo rhubarb

sal salt
salado salted, salty
salchichas sausages
salchichón salami
salmonetes red mullet
salmón salmon; **~ ahumado** smoked salmon
salsa sauce
salsa a la catalana sauce of tomato and green peppers
salsa a la vasca parsley, peas, garlic; a delicate green dressing for fish in the Basque country
salsa alioli garlic sauce
salsa de tomate ketchup
salsa en escabeche sweet and sour sauce
salsa española brown sauce with herbs, spices, and wine
salsa mayordoma butter and parsley sauce
salsa picante hot pepper sauce
salsa romana bacon/ham and egg cream sauce
salsa romesco green peppers, pimentos, garlic; popular chilled dressing for fish on the east coast around Tarragona
salsa verde parsley sauce
salteado sautéed
salvia sage
sandía watermelon
sangrita tequila with tomato, orange, and lime juices
sangría wine punch

sardinas sardines

seco dry

sencillo plain

sepia cuttlefish

serrano cured

sesos brains

setas mushrooms

sidra cider

sobrasada salami

soda soda water

sol y sombra blend of wine-distilled brandy and aniseed liqueur

solo black *(coffee)*; straight/neat

solomillo de cerdo tenderloin of pork

sopa soup; ~ **de buey** oxtail; ~ **de ajo** garlic; ~ **de arroz** rice; ~ **de camarones** shrimp; ~ **de cangrejo** crab; ~ **castellana** baked garlic; ~ **de cebolla** onion;

~ **de cocido** a kind of broth; ~ **de espárragos** asparagus; ~ **de fideos** noodle; ~ **de mariscos** seafood; ~ **de patatas** potato; ~ **de pescado** fish; ~ **de tomate** tomato; ~ **de verduras** vegetable; ~ **juliana** bouillon of finely shredded vegetables; ~ **sevillana** highly spiced fish soup

sorbete (iced) fruit drink

suave mild

suizo bun

suplemento sobre ... ...extra

surtido assorted

T

taco wheat or cornflour pancake, usually with meat filling, garnished with spicy sauce

tajada slice

tallarín noodle

tamal pastry dough of coarsely ground cornmeal with meat or fruit filling, steamed in corn-husks

tapas snacks

tarta de almendras almond tart

tarta de manzana apple tart

tarta de moka mocha cake

tarta helada ice cream cake

tartaletas small open tarts filled with fish, meat, vegetables or cheese

taza de café cup of coffee

té tea

ternera veal

tinto red

Tío Pepe brand of sherry

tipo roquefort blue *(cheese)*

tocino salted fresh lard, ~ **de panceta** bacon, ~ **entreverado** streaky bacon

tocino/tocinillo de cielo dessert of whipped egg yolks and sugar

tajunto rabbit stew

tomates tomatoes

tomillo thyme

tónica tonic water

toronja type of grapefruit

tortilla omelet; ~ **al ron** rum; ~ **de alcachofa** artichoke; ~ **de cebolla** onion; ~ **de espárragos** asparagus; ~ **de jamón** ham; ~ **de patatas** potato;

~ **de queso** cheese; ~ **de setas** mushroom; ~ **gallega** potato omelet with ham, chili;

~ paisana with potatoes, peas, prawns or ham

tortitas pancakes/waffles

tostadas toast

tripas tripe

Triple Seco orange liqueur

trucha trout; **~ a la navarra** stuffed with ham; **~ frita a la asturiana** floured and fried in butter, garnished with lemon

trufas truffles

tumbet ratatouille and potato-type casserole with meat or fish *(Maj.)*

turrón nougat

U

ulloa (queso de …) soft cheese from Galicia

uvas grapes; **~ blancas** green; **~ negras** black

uvas pasas raisins

V

vaca salada corned beef

vainilla vanilla

valenciana a type of paella, the classic version

variado varied, assorted

varios sundries

vaso glass

venado venison

veneras scallops

verduras vegetables

vermut vermouth

vieira scallop

villalón (queso de …) mild cheese

vinagreta piquant vinegar dressing

vino wine; **~ de mesa** table wine; **~ del país** local wine

(a la) vizcaína with green peppers, tomatoes, garlic, and paprika

W

whisky whisky; **~ americano** bourbon; **~ con soda** whisky and soda; **~ escocés** Scotch

X

xampaña Catalonian sparkling wine

xató olive and endive salad *(Cat.)*

Y

yema egg yolk

yemas dessert of whipped egg yolks and sugar

yogur yogurt

Z

zamorana ham, pork loin, pig's feet/trotters, chili pepper

zanahorias carrots

zarzamoras blackberries

zarzuela savory stew of assorted fish and shellfish *(Cat.)*; **~ de pescado** selection of fish with highly seasoned sauce

zumo fresh juice; **~ de fruta** fruit juice

TRAVEL

ESSENTIAL	
A ticket to …	**Un billete para …** *oon beel-yeteh para*
Two for the museum.	**Dos para el museo.** *dos para el mooseyo*
one-way [single]	**de ida** *deh eeda*
round-trip [return]	**de ida y vuelta** *deh eeda ee bwelta*
How much …?	**¿Cuánto …?** *kwanto*

SAFETY

Spain is a relatively safe country and violent crimes against tourists are rare.

Would you accompany me to the bus stop?	**¿Me acompañaría a la parada de autobús?** *meh akompañaree a la parada deh aootoboos*
I don't want to … on my own.	**No quiero … solo(-a).** *no keeyero …solo(-a)*
stay here	**quedarme aquí** *kedarmeh akee*
walk home	**ir a casa andando** *eer a kasa andando*
I don't feel safe here.	**No me siento seguro(-a) aquí.** *no meh seeyento segooro akee*

ARRIVAL

Most visitors, including citizens of all EU countries, the United States, Canada, Eire, Australia and New Zealand, require only a valid passport for entry to Spain.

Import restrictions between EU countries have been relaxed on items for personal use or consumption which are bought duty-paid within the EU. Suggested maximum: 90l. wine or 60l. sparkling wine; 20l. fortified wine, 10l. spirits, and 110l. beer.

Duty free into:	Cigarettes	Cigars	Tobacco	Spirits	Wine
Spain	200	50	250 g.	1 l.	2 l.
Canada	200 and	50 and	400 g.	1 l. or	1 l.
UK	200 or	50 or	250 g.	1 l. and	2 l.
U.S.	200 and	100 and	discretionary	1 l. or	1 l.

Passport control

We have a joint passport.	**Tenemos un pasaporte conjunto.** *tenemos oon pasaporteh konkhoonto*
The children are on this passport.	**Los niños están en este pasaporte.** *los neeños estan en esteh pasaporteh*
I'm here on vacation [holiday]/on business.	**Estoy aquí de vacaciones/en viaje de negocios.** *estoy akee deh bakathyones/ en beeyakheh deh negothyoss*
I'm just passing through.	**Estoy de paso …** *estoy deh paso*
I'm going to …	**Voy a …** *boy a*
I won't be working here.	**No voy a trabajar aquí.** *no boy a trabakhar akee*
I'm …	**Estoy …** *estoy*
on my own	**solo(-a)** *solo(-a)*
with my family	**con mi familia** *kon mee fameeleeya*
with a group	**con un grupo** *kon oon groopo*

Customs

I have only the normal allowances.	**Sólo lo normal.** *solo lo normal*

It's a gift/for my personal use.	**Es un regalo/para uso personal.** *es oon regalo/para ooso personal*
I would like to declare …	**Quiero declarar …** *keeyero deklarar*
I don't understand.	**No entiendo.** *no enteeyendo*
Does anyone here speak English?	**¿Hay alguien aquí que hable inglés?** *eye algeeyen akee keh ableh eengles*

YOU MAY HEAR

¿Tiene algo que declarar?	Do you have anything to declare?
Tiene que pagar impuestos por por esto.	You must pay duty on this.
¿Dónde compró esto?	Where did you buy this?
Abra esta bolsa por favor.	Please open this bag.
¿Tiene más equipaje?	Do you have any more luggage?

Duty-free shopping

YOU MAY SEE

ADUANAS	customs
ARTÍCULOS LIBRES DE IMPUESTOS	duty-free goods
ARTÍCULOS QUE DECLARAR	goods to declare
NADA QUE DECLARAR	nothing to declare
CONTROL DE PASAPORTES	passport control
POLICÍA	police
PASO DE LA FRONTERA	border crossing

What currency is this in?	**¿En qué moneda/divisa está esto?** *en keh moneda/deebeesa esta esto*
Can I pay in …?	**¿Puedo pagar en …?** *pwedo pagar en*
dollars/euros/pounds	**dólares/euros/libras** *dolares/eh-ooros/leebras*

PLANE

A number of private airlines, such as Air Europa and Aviaco, offer competitive prices across the internal air network and selected international flights.

Tickets and reservations

When is the … flight to Madrid?	**¿Cuándo sale el … vuelo a Madrid?** *kwando saleh el … bwelo a madreeth*
first/next/last	**primer/próximo/último** *preemer/prokseemo/oolteemo*
I'd like 2 … tickets to Madrid.	**Quiero dos billetes … a Madrid.** *keeyero dos beel-yetehs … a madreeth*
one-way [single]	**de ida** *deh eeda*
round-trip [return]	**de ida y vuelta** *deh eeda ee bwelta*
first class	**de primera clase** *deh preemera klaseh*
business class	**de clase preferente** *deh klaseh preferenteh*
economy class	**económico** *ekonomeeko*
How much is a flight to …?	**¿Cuánto cuesta un vuelo a …?** *kwanto kwesta oon bwelo a*
Are there any supplements/ reductions?	**¿Tienen algúnos suplementos/descuentos?** *teeyenen algoonos sooplementos/deskwentos*
I'd like to … my reservation for flight number …	**Quiero … mi reserva del vuelo número …** *keeyero … mee reserba del bwelo noomero*
cancel	**cancelar** *kanthelar*
change	**cambiar** *kambeeyar*
confirm	**confirmar** *konfeermar*

Inquiries about the flight

How long is the flight?	**¿Cuánto dura el vuelo?** *kwanto doora el bwelo*
What time does the plane leave?	**¿A qué hora sale el avión?** *a keh ora saleh el abeeyon*
What time will we arrive?	**¿A qué hora llegamos?** *a keh ora l-yegamos*
What time do I have to check in?	**¿A qué hora tengo que facturar?** *a keh ora tengo keh faktoorar*

Checking in

Where is the check-in counter for flight …?	**¿Dónde está el mostrador de facturación del vuelo …?** _dondeh esta el mostrador deh faktooratheeyon del bwelo_
I have …	**Tengo …** _tengo_
three suitcases to check in	**tres maletas para facturar** _tres maletas para faktoorar_
two carry-ons	**dos bultos de mano** _dos booltos deh mano_
How much baggage is allowed free?	**¿Cuánto equipaje está permitido sin pagar?** _kwanto ekeepakeh esta permeeteedo seen pagar_

YOU MAY HEAR

¿Quiere un asiento que dé a la ventana o al pasillo?	Would you like a window or an aisle seat?
¿Fumador o no fumador?	Smoking or non-smoking?
Por favor, pase a la sala de embarque.	Please go through to the departure lounge.
¿Cuántos bultos de equipaje tiene?	How many pieces of baggage do you have?
Lleva exceso de equipaje.	You have excess baggage.
Tendrá que pagar un suplemento de … euros por kilo de equipaje en exceso.	You'll have to pay a supplement of … euros per kilo of excess baggage.
Eso pesa demasiado/eso es demasiado grande para pasar como equipaje de mano.	That's too heavy/large for carry-on [hand laggage].
¿Hizo las maletas usted?	Did you pack these bags yourself?
¿Contienen algún artículo punzante o eléctrico?	Do they contain any sharp or electronic items?

YOU MAY SEE

LLEGADAS	arrivals
SALIDAS	departures
NO DEJE SU EQUIPAJE DESATENDIDO	do not leave bags unattended
REVISIÓN DE SEGURIDAD	security check

Information

Is there any delay on flight ...?	**¿Lleva retraso el vuelo ...?** *l-yeba retraso el bwelo*
How late will it be?	**¿Cuánto tiempo lleva de retraso?** *kwanto teeyempo l-yeba deh retraso*
Has the flight from ... landed?	**¿Ha aterrizado el vuelo procedente de ...?** *a aterreethado el bwelo prothedenteh deh*
Which gate does flight ... leave from?	**¿De qué puerta sale el vuelo ...?** *deh keh pwerta saleh el bwelo*

Boarding

Your boarding card, please.	**Su tarjeta de embarque, por favor.** *soo tarkheta deh embarkeh por fabor*
Could I have a drink/something to eat, please?	**¿Podría tomar algo de beber/comer, por favor?** *podreeya tomar algo deh beber/komer por fabor*
Please wake me for the meal.	**Por favor, despiérteme para la comida.** *por fabor despeeyertemeh para la komeeda*
What time will we arrive?	**¿A qué hora llegaremos?** *a keh ora l-yegaremos*
An airsickness bag, please.	**Una bolsa para el mareo por favor.** *oona bolsa para el mareyo por fabor*

Arrival

Where is/are the ...?	**¿Dónde está/están ...?** *dondeh esta/estan*
currency exchange	**la ventanilla de cambio** *la bentaneel-ya deh kambeeyo*
buses	**los autobuses** *los aootobooses*
car rental [hire]	**el alquiler de coches** *el alkeeler deh koches*
exit	**la salida** *la saleeda*
taxis	**los taxis** *los taksees*
telephones	**los teléfonos** *los telefonos*
Is there a bus into town?	**¿Hay un autobús que va a la ciudad?** *eye oon aootoboos keh ba a la theeyoodath*
How do I get to the ... Hotel?	**¿Cómo se va al Hotel ...?** *komo seh ba al otel*

Baggage

Tipping: €1 per bag.

Porter! Excuse me!	**¡Mozo! ¡Disculpe!** _motho. deeskoolpeh_
Could you take my luggage to …?	**¿Podría llevar mi equipaje a …?** _podreeya l-yebar mee ekeepakheh a_
a taxi/bus	**un taxi/autobús** oòn _taksee/aootoboos_
Where is/are (the) …?	**¿Dónde está/están …?** _dondeh esta/estan_
luggage carts [trolleys]	**los carritos para el equipaje** _los karreetos para el ekeepakheh_
luggage lockers	**las taquillas** _las takeel-yas_
baggage check	**la consigna** _la konseegna_
Where is the luggage from flight …?	**¿Dónde está el equipaje del vuelo …?** _dondeh esta el ekeepakheh del bwelo_

Loss, damage, and theft

My baggage has been lost/stolen.	**Han perdido/robado mi equipaje.** _an perdeedo/rrobado mee ekeepakheh_
My suitcase was damaged in transit.	**Mi maleta se ha estropeado en el tránsito.** _mee maleta seh a estropeyado en el transeeto_
Our baggage has not arrived.	**Nuestro equipaje no ha llegado.** _nwestro ekeepakheh no a l-yegado_
Do you have claim forms?	**¿Tienen formularios para reclamaciones?** _teeyenen formoolareeoss para rreklamatheeoness_

YOU MAY HEAR

¿Puede describir su equipaje?	What does your baggage look like?
¿Tiene la etiqueta de recogida?	Do you have the claim check [reclaim tag]?
Su equipaje …	Your luggage …
puede que lo hayan mandado a …	may have been sent to …
puede que llegue hoy más tarde	may arrive later today
Vuelva usted mañana, por favor.	Please come back tomorrow.
Llame a este número para comprobar que su equipaje ha llegado.	Call this number to check if your baggage has arrived.

TRAIN

On Spain's rail network **RENFE (Red Nacional de los Ferrocarriles Españoles)** children under 4 travel free; children aged 4–12 pay half fare.

Check out the various reductions and travel cards available. Rates are cheaper on "off days" (**días azules**). Some travel cards can also be used for local buses and subway. Another way is to buy tickets in a "checkbook" from travel agents. These can be exchanged for train tickets at special rates on "off days."

Tickets can be purchased and reservations made in travel agencies or at railway stations. The purchase of a ticket usually means that you are allocated a seat. You can reserve seats in advance. For longer trips there is a smoking car, otherwise the train is non-smoking.

AVE _abeh_
High-speed train (**alta velocidad española**), operating between Madrid and Seville, and taking just two hours.

EuroCity _e-oorotheetee_
International express, first and second classes.

Talgo, Electrotren, TER _talgo, elektrotren, tehr_
Luxury diesels, first and second classes; supplementary charge over the regular fare; seats should be reserved in advance. Similar services are provided by **Intercity** and **Tren Estrella**.

Expreso, Rápido _ekspresso, rrapeedo_
Long-distance expresses; stopping at all main towns.

Omnibus, Tranvía, Automotor _omneeboos, tranbeea, awtomotor_
Local train; making frequent stops.

Auto Expreso _awto ekspresso_
Car train; you can load your car and travel in a sleeper car; reductions available on the **auto expreso** if more than one berth reserved.

Coche cama _kocheh kama_
Sleeping car; compartments with wash basins and one or two berths. A cheaper way of sleeping during your trip is to buy a **litera,** one of the berths in a compartment of six.

Coche comedor _kocheh komedor_
Dining car; generally included on overnight trips. Otherwise, there may be a buffet car; lunch served at your seats on certain trains; or simply a sandwich and drinks car on shorter trips.

Furgón de equipajes _foorgon deh ekeepakhess_
Baggage car [van]; only registered baggage permitted.

To the station

How do I get to the train station?	**¿Cómo se llega a la estación de trenes?** *komo seh l-yega a la estatheeyon deh trenes*
Do trains to León leave from … Station?	**¿Salen de la estación … los trenes a León?** *salen deh la estatheeyon … los trenes a leyon*
How far is it?	**¿A qué distancia está?** *a keh deestantheeya esta*
Can I leave my car there?	**¿Puedo dejar mi coche allí?** *pwedo dekhar mee kocheh al-yee*

At the station

Where is/are …?	**¿Dónde está/están …?** *dondeh esta/estan*
currency exchange office	**la oficina de cambio de moneda** *la ofeetheena deh kambeeyo deh moneda*
information desk	**la ventanilla de información** *la bentaneel-ya deh eenformatheeyon*
baggage check	**la consigna** *la konseegna*
lost and found [lost property office]	**la oficina de objetos perdidos** *la ofeetheena deh obkhetos perdeedos*
luggage lockers	**las taquillas** *las takeel-yas*
platforms	**los andenes** *los andenes*
snack bar	**el bar** *el bar*
ticket office	**el despacho de billetes** *el despacho deh beel-yetes*
waiting room	**la sala de espera** *la sala deh espera*

YOU MAY SEE

A LOS ANDENES	to the platforms
ENTRADA	entrance
SALIDA	exit
INFORMACIÓN	information
RESERVAS	reservations
LLEGADAS	arrivals
SALIDAS	departures

Tickets

I'd like a ... ticket to Toledo.	**Quiero un billete ... a Toledo.** *keeyero oon beel-yeteh ... a toledo*
one-way [single]	**de ida** *deh eeda*
round-trip [return]	**de ida y vuelta** *deh eeda ee bwelta*
first/second class	**de primera/segunda clase** *deh preemera/segoonda klaseh*
concessionary	**con descuento** *kon deskwento*
I'd like to reserve a seat.	**Quiero reservar una plaza.** *keeyero reserbar oona platha*
I'd like to reserve a(n) ...	**Quiero reservar ...** *oon aseeyento keh deh al paseel-yo*
aisle seat/window seat	**un asiento que dé al pasillo/a la ventana** *oon aseeyento keh deh al paseel-yo/ a la bentana*
I'd like to reserve a berth.	**Quiero reservar un camarote.** *keeyero reserbar oona leetera*
Is there a sleeping car?	**¿Hay coche cama?** *eye kocheh kama*
I'd like a(n) ... berth.	**Quiero una litera ...** *keeyero oona leetera*
upper/lower	**de arriba/abajo** *deh arreeba/abakho*
Can I buy a ticket on board?	**¿Puedo comprar un billete dentro del tren?** *pwedo komprar oon beel-yeteh dentro del tren*

Price

How much is that?	**¿Cuánto es?** *kwanto es*
Is there a discount for ...?	**¿Hacen descuento a ...?** *athen deskwento a*
children/families	**los niños/las familias** *los neeños/las fameeleeyas*
senior citizens	**los pensionistas** *los penseeyoneestas*
students	**los estudiantes** *los estoodeeyantes*
Do you offer a cheap same-day round-trip [return] ticket?	**¿Tienen una oferta por un billete de ida y vuelta en el mismo día?** *teeyenen oona oferta por oon beel-yeteh deh eeda ee bwelta en el meesmo deeya*

Queries

Do I have to change trains? **¿Tengo que cambiar de trenes?** *tengo keh kambeeyar deh trenes*

Is it a direct train? **¿Es un tren directo?** *es oon tren deerekto*

You have to change at … **Tiene que cambiar en …** *teeyeneh keh kambeeyar en*

How long is this ticket valid? **¿Para cuánto tiempo vale este billete?** *para kwanto teeyempo baleh esteh beel-yeteh*

Can I take my bicycle on the train? **¿Puedo llevar mi bicicleta en el tren?** *pwedo l-yebar mee beetheekleta en el tren*

Can I return on the same ticket? **¿Puedo volver con el mismo billete?** *pwedo bolber kon el meesmo beel-yeteh*

In which car [coach] is my seat? **¿En qué compartimento está mi asiento?** *en keh komparteemento esta mee aseeyento*

Is there a dining car on the train? **¿Hay coche restaurante en el tren?** *eyo kocheh restawranteh en el tren*

Train times

Could I have a timetable, please? **¿Podría darme un horario (de trenes), por favor?** *podreeya darmeh oon orareeyo (deh trenes) por fabor*

When is the … train to Vigo? **¿Cuándo sale el … tren a Vigo?** *kwando saleh el … tren a beego*

first/next/last **primer/próximo/último** *preemer/prokseemo/oolteemo*

IN A TRAIN STATION

Dos billetes a Toledo, por favor. *dos beelyetehs a toledo por fabor* (Two tickets to Toledo, please.)

¿De ida o de ida y vuelta? *deh eehda o deh eehda ee bwelta* (One way or round trip?)

De ida y vuelta, por favor. *deh eehda ee bwelta por fabor* (Round trip, please.)

How frequent are trains to …?	**¿Con qué frecuencia salen los trenes a …?**
	kon keh frekwentheeya salen los trenes a
once/twice a day	**una/dos veces al día**
	oona/dos bethes al deeya
5 times a day	**cinco veces al día**
	theenko bethes al deeya
every hour	**cada hora** *kada ora*
What time do they leave?	**¿A qué hora salen?**
	a keh ora salen
on the hour	**a la hora en punto**
	a la ora en poonto
20 minutes past the hour	**a las … y veinte**
	a las … ee baynteh
What time does the train stop/arrive in …?	**¿A qué hora para/llega el tren a …?**
	a keh ora para/l-yega el tren a
How long is the trip [journey]?	**¿Cuánto dura el viaje?**
	kwanto doora el beeyakheh
Is the train on time?	**¿Llega puntual el tren?**
	l-yega poontoowal el tren

Departures

Which platform does the train to … leave from?	**¿De qué andén sale el tren a …?**
	deh keh anden saleh el tren a
Where is platform 4?	**¿Dónde está el andén cuatro?**
	dondeh esta el anden kwatro
over there	**allí** *al-yee*
on the left/right	**a la izquierda/derecha**
	a la eethkeeyerda/derecha
under the underpass	**debajo del pasaje subterráneo**
	debakho del pasakheh soobterraneyo
Where do I change for …?	**¿Dónde tengo que cambiar para …?**
	dondeh tengo keh kambeeyar para
How long will I have to wait for a connection?	**¿Cuánto tiempo tengo que esperar para un enlace?** *kwanto teeyempo tengo keh esperar para oon enlatheh*

Boarding

Is this the right platform for the train to …?	**¿Es éste el andén para el tren a …?** *es esteh el anden para el tren a*
Is this the train to …?	**¿Es éste el tren a …?** *es esteh el tren a*
Is this seat taken?	**¿Está ocupado este asiento?** *esta okoopado esteh aseeyento*
I think that's my seat.	**Creo que ése es mi asiento.** *kreyo keh eseh es mee aseeyento*
Here's my reservation.	**Aquí tengo la reserva.** *akee tengo la rreserba*
Are there any seats/berths available?	**¿Hay asientos/literas libres?** *eye aseeyentos/leeteras leebres*
Do you mind if …?	**¿Le importa si …?** *leh eemporta see*
I sit here	**me siento aquí** *meh seeyento akee*
I open the window	**abro la ventana** *abro la bentana*

During the trip

How long are we stopping here?	**¿Por cuánto tiempo paramos aquí?** *por kwanto teeyempo paramos akee*
When do we get to …?	**¿Cuándo llegamos a …?** *kwando l-yegamos a*
Have we passed …?	**¿Hemos pasado …?** *emos pasado*
Where is the dining/sleeping car?	**¿Dónde está el coche restaurante/cama?** *dondeh esta el kocheh restawranteh/kama*
Where is my berth?	**¿Dónde está mi litera?** *dondeh esta mee leetera*
I've lost my ticket.	**He perdido el billete.** *eh perdeedo el beel-yeteh*

YOU MAY SEE

FRENO DE EMERGENCIA	emergency brake
PUERTAS AUTOMÁTICAS	automatic doors

LONG-DISTANCE BUS [COACH]

Long-distance buses are good if you want to visit out-of-the-way places. Most buses only serve towns and villages within a region or province. From larger cities you can book cross-country and international lines – information is available from the local central bus station (**estación de autobuses**).

Where is the bus [coach] station?	**¿Dónde está la estación de autobuses?** _dondeh esta la estatheeyon deh awtobooses_
When's the next bus [coach] to …?	**¿Cuándo sale el próximo autobús a …?** _kwando saleh el prokseemo awtoboos a_
Where does it leave from?	**¿De qué andén sale?** _deh keh anden saleh_
Where are the bus [coach] stops?	**¿Dónde están los andenes?** _dondeh estan los andenes_
Does the bus [coach] stop at …?	**¿Para el autobús en …?** _para el awtoboos en_
How long does the trip [journey] take?	**¿Cuánto dura el viaje?** _kwanto doora el beeyakheh_

YOU MAY SEE

PARADA DE AUTOBUSES	bus stop
PARADA SOLICITADA	request stop
PROHIBIDO FUMAR	no smoking
SALIDA DE EMERGENCIA	(emergency) exit

BUS

In most buses you pay as you enter. For larger cities with fixed fares, a 10-trip pass (**un bonobús**) is cheapest – but remember to use the cancelling machine by the driver for each trip. These tickets are sold at newspaper stands in Madrid; at banks in Barcelona, lottery-ticket shops and metro stations.

Where is the bus station [terminus]?	**¿Dónde está la estación de autobuses?** _dondeh esta la estatheeyon deh awtobooses_
Where can I get a bus to …?	**¿Dónde se coge un autobús a …?** _dondeh se kokheh oon awtoboos a …_

YOU MAY HEAR

Tiene que tomar el autobús número …	You need bus number …
Tiene que cambiar de autobús en …	You must change buses at …

Buying tickets

Where can I buy tickets?	**¿Dónde se puede comprar billetes?** _dondeh seh pwedeh komprar beel-yetes_
A … ticket to…	**Un billete … para…** _oon beel-yeteh … para_
one-way [single]	**de ida** _deh eeda_
round-trip [return]	**de ida y vuelta** _deh eeda ee bwelta_
multiple trip	**bonobús** _bonoboos_
day/weekly/monthly	**para todo el día/la semana/el mes** _para todo el deeya/la semana/el mes_
How much is the fare to …?	**¿Cuánto cuesta el billete a …?** _kwanto kwesta el beel-yeteh a_

YOU MAY SEE

PIQUE SU BILLETE	validate your ticket

Traveling

Is this the right bus to …?	**¿Es éste el autobús a …?** _es este el awtoboos a_
Could you tell me when to get off?	**¿Podría decirme cuándo me tengo que bajar?** _podreeya detheermeh kwando meh tengo keh bakhar_
Do I have to change buses?	**¿Tengo que hacer transbordo?** _tengo keh ather transbordo_
How many stops are there to …?	**¿Cuántas paradas hay hasta …?** _kwantas paradas eye asta_
Next stop please!	**¡Próxima parada, por favor!** _prokseema parada por fabor_

AT A BUS STOP

¿Es éste el autobús al centro? _es este el awtoboos al thentro_ (Is this the bus to downtown?)

Sí, es el número ocho. _see es el noomero ocho_ (Yes, bus number 8.)

Muchas gracias. _moochas gratheeyas_ (Thank you very much.)

De nada. _de nada_ (You're welcome.)

SUBWAY [METRO]

There are extensive subway [metro] systems in Madrid and Barcelona, with a striking new system in Bilbao. Big maps outside each station make the systems easy to use. Cheaper ten-ride tickets (**billete de diez viajes**) are available.

Barcelona offers **un bon-bus T1**, which allows travel on both the metro and the bus networks.

Most metro systems close at 11 p.m. on weekdays and at 1 a.m. on Saturdays.

General inquiries

Where's the nearest subway [metro] station?	**¿Dónde está la próxima estación de metro?** _dondeh esta la prokseema estatheeyon deh metro_
Where do I buy a ticket?	**¿Dónde se compran los billetes?** _dondeh seh kompran los beel-yetes_
Could I have a map of the subway [metro]?	**¿Podría darme un mapa del metro?** _podreeya darmeh oon mapa del metro_

Traveling

Which line should I take for …?	**¿Qué línea tengo que coger para …?** _keh leenaya tengo keh kokher para_
Is this the right train for …?	**¿Es éste el tren para …?** _es esteh el tren para_
Which stop is it for …?	**¿Qué parada es la de …?** _keh parada es la deh_
How many stops is it to …?	**¿Cuántas paradas quedan para …?** _kwantas paradas kedan para_
Is the next stop …?	**¿Es … la próxima parada?** _es … la prokseema parada_
Where are we?	**¿Dónde estamos?** _dondeh estamos_
Where do I change for …?	**¿Dónde tengo que hacer transbordo para …?** _dondeh tengo keh ather transbordo para_

YOU MAY SEE

A OTRAS LÍNEAS/ CORRESPONDENCIA	to other lines/ transfer

FERRY

Regular ferry services are run to the Balearic Islands (from Valencia) and Canary Islands (by **Compañía Transmediterránea SA**).

Why not spend the day in Africa? A ferry trip to Tangiers (Morocco) and Ceuta (Spanish territory) operates from Algeciras.

When is the car ferry to …?	**¿Cuándo sale el ferry a …?** _kwan_do _sa_leh el _fe_rree a
first/next/last	**primer/próximo/último** _pree_mer/_prok_seemo/_ool_teemo
hovercraft/ship	**el aerodeslizador/el barco** el aeyrodesleetha_dor_/el _bar_ko
A round-trip [return] ticket for …	**Un billete de ida y vuelta para …** oon beel-_ye_teh deh _ee_da ee _bwel_ta _pa_ra
one car and one trailer [caravan]	**un coche y una roulotte** oon _ko_cheh ee _oo_na roo_lo_teh
two adults and three children	**dos adultos y tres niños** dos a_dool_tos ee tres _nee_ños
I want to reserve a … cabin.	**Quiero reservar un camarote …** kee_ye_ro reser_bar_ oon kama_ro_teh
single/double	**individual/doble** eendeebeedoo_wal_/_dob_leh

---

YOU MAY SEE

BOTE SALVAVIDAS	life boat
PROHIBIDO EL ACCESO	no access
PUNTO DE REUNIÓN	muster station
SALVAVIDAS	life preserver [life belt]

BOAT TRIPS

Is there a …?	**¿Hay …?** eye
boat trip/river cruise	**una excursión en barco/un crucero por** **el río** _oo_na ekskoorsee_yon_ en _bar_ko/ oon kroo_the_ro por el _ree_yo
What time does it leave/return?	**¿A qué hora sale/vuelve?** a keh _o_ra _sa_leh/_bwel_veh
Where can we buy tickets?	**¿Dónde se compran los billetes?** _don_deh seh _kom_pran los beel-_ye_tes

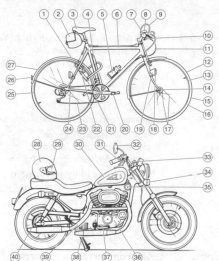

1	brake pad **frenos** mpl	22	generator [dynamo] **dínamo** m
2	bicycle bag **cesta** f	23	chain **cadena** f
3	saddle **sillín** m	24	rear light **luz** f **trasera**
4	pump **bomba** f	25	rim **llanta** f
5	water bottle **botella** f **para el agua**	26	reflectors **reflectores** mpl
6	frame **cuadro** m	27	fender [mudguard] **guardabarros** mpl
7	handlebars **manillar** m		
8	bell **timbre** m	28	helmet **casco** m
9	brake cable **cable** m **de los frenos**	29	visor **visor** m
10	gear shift [lever] **palanca** f **para cambiar de marcha**	30	fuel tank **depósito** m **del combustible**
11	gear control cable **cable** m **de las marchas/de control**	31	clutch **palanca** f **del embrague**
12	inner tube **cámara** f	32	mirror **espejo** m
13	front/back wheel **rueda** f **delantera/trasera**	33	ignition switch **interruptor** m **de arranque**
14	axle **eje** m	34	turn signal [indicator] **intermitente** m
15	tire [tyre] **neumático** m	35	horn **cláxon** m
16	wheel **rueda** f	36	engine **motor** m
17	spokes **radio** m	37	gear shift [lever] **palanca** f **para las marchas**
18	bulb **luz** f		
19	headlamp **luz** f **delantera**	38	kick stand [main stand] **pie** m
20	pedal **pedal** m	39	exhaust pipe **tubo** m **de escape**
21	lock **candado** m	40	chain guard **protector** m **de la cadena**

BICYCLE/MOTORBIKE

I'd like to rent a …	**Quiero alquilar …** *keeyero alkeelar* **una**
3-/10-speed bicycle	**bicicleta de tres/diez marchas** *oona beetheekleta deh tres/deeyeth marchas*
mountain bike	**una bicicleta de montaña** *oona beetheekleta deh montaña*
moped	**un ciclomotor** *oon theeklomotor*
motorbike	**una moto** *oona moto*
How much does it cost per day/week?	**¿Cuánto cuesta por día/semana?** *kwanto kwesta por deeya/semana*
Do you require a deposit?	**¿Hay que pagar un depósito?** *eye keh pagar oon deposito*
The brakes don't work.	**Los frenos no funcionan.** *los frenos no foontheeyonan*
There are no lights.	**No hay luces.** *no eye loothes*
The front/rear tire [tyre] has a flat [puncture].	**El neumático delantero/trasero está pinchado.** *el neyoomateeko delantero/trasero esta peenchado*

HITCHHIKING

Where are you heading?	**¿Adónde se dirige?** *adondeh seh deereekheh*
I'm heading for …	**Me dirijo a …** *meh deereekho a*
Can you give me/us a lift?	**¿Me/nos puede llevar?** *meh/nos pwedeh l-yebar*
Is that on the way to …?	**¿Está de camino a …?** *esta deh kameeno a*
Could you drop me off …?	**¿Me podría dejar …?** *meh podreeya dekhar*
here	**aquí** *akee*
at the … exit	**a la salida …** *a la saleeda*
downtown	**en el centro** *en el thentro*
Thanks for the lift.	**Gracias por traernos.** *gratheeyas por trayernos*

TAXI/CAB

Taxis are marked **SP** (**servicio público**) and a green sign indicates **libre** when free; in tourist areas they are often unmetered, though fares to most destinations are fixed and displayed at the main taxi stand.

Tipping: 10% for the taxi driver.

Where can I get a taxi?	**¿Dónde puedo coger un taxi?** _dondeh_ _pwe_do _ko_kher oon _tak_see
Do you have the number for a taxi service?	**¿Tiene el número de alguna empresa de taxi?** _teeye_neh el _noo_mero deh _al_goona em_pre_sa deh _tak_see
I'd like a taxi …	**Quiero un taxi …** _keeye_ro oon _tak_see
now	**ahora** _a-o_ra
in an hour	**dentro de una hora** _den_tro deh _oo_na _o_ra
for tomorrow at 9:00	**para mañana a las nueve** _para_ mañana a las _nwe_beh
The pick-up address is …	**La dirección es …** la deerekthee_yon_ es
I'm going to …	**Me dirijo a …** meh dee_ree_kho a
Please take me to …	**Por favor, lléveme a …** por fa_bor_ _l-ye_bemeh a
airport/train station	**el aeropuerto/la estación de trenes** el ayro_pwer_to/la estathee_yon_ deh _tre_nes
this address	**esta dirección** _es_ta deerekthee_yon_
How much will it cost?	**¿Cuánto costará?** _kwan_to kosta_ra_
How much is that?	**¿Cuánto es?** _kwan_to es
You said … euros.	**Dijo … euros.** _dee_kho … eh-oo_ros_
Keep the change.	**Quédese con el cambio.** _ke_deseh kon el _kam_beeyo

---

AT A TAXI STAND

¿Cuánto costará al aeropuerto? _kwan_to kosta_ra_ al ayro_pwer_to (*How much is it to the airport?*)
Quince euros. _keen_theh eh-oo_ros_ (*15 euros.*)
Gracias. _gra_theeyas (*Thank you.*)

CAR/AUTOMOBILE

The minimum driving age is 18. While driving, the following documents must be carried at all times: driver's license, vehicle registration document and insurance documentation. If you don't hold an EU license, an international driving permit is also required. Insurance for minimum third party risks is compulsory in Europe. It is recommended that you take out international motor insurance (Green Card insurance) through your insurer.

The most common crime against tourists in Spain is theft from rental cars. Always look for secure parking areas overnight and never leave valuables in your car at any time.

Essential equipment: warning triangle, national identity (country of origin) sticker, and a set of spare head- and rear-lamp bulbs. Seat belts are compulsory. Children under 10 must travel in the rear.

Traffic on main roads has priority; where 2 roads of equal importance merge, traffic from the right has priority. Tolls are payable on certain roads, they can be high.

Traffic police can give hefty on-the-spot fines. A **boletín de denuncia** is issued, specifying the offense; guidelines in English for an appeal appear on the back.

The use of horns is prohibited in built-up areas except for emergencies.

Alcohol limit in blood: max. 80mg/100ml.

Road network

A (**autopista**) – toll highway [motorway] (blue sign), and (**autovías**) – free highway [motorway] (green sign); **N** (**nacional**) – main road; **C** (**comarcal**) – secondary road (white sign); **V** (**vecinal**) – local road (prefixed by letter denoting province)

Conversion Chart													
km	1	10	20	30	40	50	60	70	80	90	100	110	120	130
miles	0.62	6	12	19	25	31	37	44	50	56	62	68	74	81

Speed limits	Residential	Built-up area	Main road	Highway/motorway
	kmh (mph)	*kmh (mph)*	*kmh (mph)*	*kmh (mph)*
Cars	20 (12)	50 (31)	90-100 (56-62)	120 (74)

Gas [Petrol]	Leaded	Lead-free	Diesel
	Normal (92)	Sin plomo (95)	Gasóleo 'A' (98)

Car rental

Third-party insurance is included in the basic charge, usually with Collision Damage Waiver.

The minimum age varies from 21 if paying by credit card, 23 if paying by cash. In the latter case, a large deposit will be charged.

Where can I rent a car?	**¿Dónde puedo alquilar un coche?** *dondeh pwedo alkeelar oon kocheh*
I'd like to rent …	**Quiero alquilar …** *keeyero alkeelar*
2-/4-door car	**un coche de dos/cuatro puertas** *oon kocheh deh dos/kwatro pwertas*
an automatic	**un coche automático** *oon kocheh aootomateeko*
a car with 4-wheel drive	**un coche con tracción a las cuatro ruedas** *oon kocheh kon traktheeyon a las kwatro roowedas*
a car with air conditioning	**un coche con aire acondicionado** *oon kocheh kon ayreh akondeetheeyonado*
I'd like it for a day/week.	**Lo quiero para un día/una semana.** *lo keeyero para oon deeya/oona semana*
How much does it cost per day/week?	**¿Cuánto cuesta por día/semana?** *kwanto kwesta por deeya/semana*
Is mileage/insurance included?	**¿Va el kilometraje/seguro incluido?** *ba el keelometrakheh/segooro eenklooweedo*
Are there special weekend rates?	**¿Tienen precios especiales de fin de semana?** *teeyenen pretheeyos espetheeyales deh feen deh semana*
Can I return the car at …?	**¿Puedo dejar el coche en …?** *pwedo dekhar el kocheh en*
What kind of fuel does it take?	**¿Qué tipo de combustible gasta?** *keh teepo deh komboosteebleh gasta*
Where is the high [full]/ low [dipped] beam ?	**¿Dónde están las largas/cortas?** *dondeh estan las largas/kortas*
Could I have full insurance?	**¿Podría hacerme un seguro a todo riesgo?** *podreeya athermeh oon segooro a todo rreeyesgo*

Gas [Petrol] station

Where's the next gas [petrol] station, please?	**¿Dónde está la próxima gasolinera, por favor?** _dondeh esta la prokseema gasoleenera por fabor_
Is it self-service?	**¿Es de autoservicio?** _es deh owtoserbeetheeyo_
Fill it up, please.	**Lleno, por favor.** _l-yeno por fabor_
… liters of gasoline, please.	**… litros de gasolina, por favor.** _… leetros deh gasoleena por fabor_
premium [super]/regular	**súper/normal** _sooper/normal_
lead-free/diesel	**sin plomo/diesel** _seen plomo/dee-ehsel_
Where is the air pump/water?	**¿Dónde está el aire/agua?** _dondeh esta el ayreh/agwa_

YOU MAY SEE

PRECIO POR LITRO	price per liter

Parking

Metered parking is common in most towns; some take credit cards as well as coins. In certain zones of Madrid, prepaid slips (**tarjeta de aparcamiento**) are required, available from tobacconists.

It is an offense to park facing against the traffic.

Vehicles that are illegally parked may be towed away (**grúa**); you will find a yellow triangle with your license plate number and address of the car-pound.

Is there a parking lot [car park] nearby?	**¿Hay un aparcamiento cerca?** _eye oon aparkameeyento therka_
What's the charge per hour/per day?	**¿Cuánto cobran por hora/día?** _kwanto kobran por ora/deeya_
Do you have some change for the parking meter?	**¿Tienen cambio para el parquímetro?** _teeyenen kambeeyo para el parkeemetro_
My car has been booted [clamped]. Who do I call?	**A mi coche le han puesto el cepo. ¿A quién llamo?** _a mee kocheh leh an pwesto el thepo. a keeyen l-yamo_

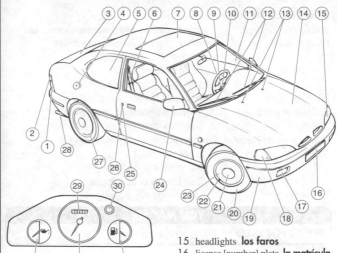

15 headlights **los faros**

16 license [number] plate **la matrícula**

17 fog lamp **el faro antiniebla**

18 turn signals [indicators] **los intermitentes**

19 bumper **el parachoques**

20 tires [tyres] **las llantas**

21 wheel cover [hubcap] **el tapacubos**

22 valve **la válvula**

23 wheels **las ruedas**

24 outside [wing] mirror **el espejo lateral**

25 automatic locks [central locking] **el cierre centralizado**

26 lock **el seguro [la cerradura]**

27 wheel rim **el rin de la rueda**

28 exhaust pipe **el tubo de escape**

29 odometer [milometer] **el cuentakilómetros**

30 warning light **la luz de advertencia**

1 taillights [back lights] **las luces traseras**

2 brakelights **las luces de los frenos**

3 trunk [boot] **el maletero**

4 gas tank door [petrol cap] **la tapa del depósito de gasolina**

5 window **la ventana**

6 seat belt **el cinturón de seguridad**

7 sunroof **el techo solar**

8 steering wheel **el volante**

9 ignition **el encendido**

10 ignition key **la llave (de encendido)**

11 windshield [windscreen] **el parabrisas**

12 windshield [windscreen] wipers **las escobillas**

13 windshield [windscreen] washer **el limpiaparabrisas**

14 hood [bonnet] **el capó**

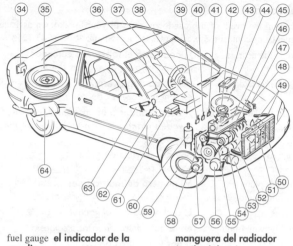

31 fuel gauge **el indicador de la gasolina**
32 speedometer **el velocímetro**
33 oil gauge **el indicador del nivel de aceite**
34 backup [reversing] lights **las luces de marcha atrás**
35 spare tire **la rueda de repuesto**
36 choke **el estárter**
37 heater **la calefacción**
38 steering column **la columna de dirección**
39 accelerator **el acelerador**
40 pedal **el pedal**
41 clutch **el embrague**
42 carburetor **el carburador**
43 battery **la batería**
44 air filter **el filtro de agua**
45 camshaft **el árbol de levas**
46 alternator **el alternador**
47 distributor **el distribuidor**
48 points **las tomas de corriente**
49 radiator hose (top/bottom) **la**

manguera del radiador (arriba/abajo)
50 radiator **el radiador**
51 fan **el ventilador**
52 engine **el motor**
53 oil filter **el filtro de aceite**
54 starter motor **el motor de arranque**
55 fan belt **la correa del ventilador**
56 horn **la bocina [el pito]**
57 brake pads **las pastillas de los frenos**
58 transmission [gearbox] **la caja de cambio**
59 brakes **los frenos**
60 shock absorbers **los amortiguadores**
61 fuses **los fusibles**
62 gear shift [lever] **la palanca de cambios**
63 handbrake **el freno de mano**
64 muffler [silencer] **el silenciador**

Breakdown

For help in the event of a breakdown: refer to your breakdown assistance documents; or contact the breakdown service: Spain: ☎ (91) 742 1213.

Where is the nearest garage?	**¿Dónde está el taller más cercano?** _dondeh esta el tal-yer mas therkano_
I've had a breakdown.	**He tenido una avería.** _eh teneedo oona abereeya_
Can you send a mechanic/ tow [breakdown] truck?	**¿Puede mandar a un mecánico/una grúa?** _pwedeh mandar a oon mekaneeko/oona groowa_
I belong to … . rescue service	**Soy del servicio de grúa …** _soy del serbeetheeyo deh groowa_
My license plate [registration] number is …	**Mi número de matrícula es …** _mee noomero deh matreekoola es_
The car is …	**El coche está …** _el kocheh esta_
on the highway [motorway]	**en la autopista** _en la aootopeesta_
2 km from …	**a dos kilómetros de …** _a dos keelometros deh_
How long will you be?	**¿Cuánto tiempo tardará?** _kwanto teeyempo tardara_

What's wrong?

I don't know what's wrong.	**No sé qué le pasa.** _no seh ke leh pasa_
My car won't start.	**Mi coche no arranca.** _mee kocheh no arranka_
The battery is dead.	**La batería no funciona.** _la batereeya no foontheeyona_
I've run out of gas [petrol].	**Se me ha acabado la gasolina.** _seh meh a akabado la gasoleena_
I have a flat [puncture].	**Tengo un pinchazo.** _tengo oon peenchatho_
There is something wrong with …	**Algo va mal en …** _algo ba mal en_
I've locked the keys in the car.	**Me he dejado las llaves en el coche.** _meh eh dekhado las l-yabes en el kocheh_

Repairs

Do you do repairs?	**¿Hacen reparaciones?** _athen reparatheeyones_
Could you have a look at my car?	**¿Podrían echarle un vistazo al coche?** _podreeyan echarleh oon beestatho al kocheh_
Can you repair it (temporarily)?	**¿Puede hacerle una reparación (provisional)?** _pwedeh atherle oona reparatheeyon (probeeseeyonal)_
Please make only essential repairs.	**Por favor, hágale reparaciones básicas solamente.** _por fabor agaleh reparatheeyones baseekas solamenteh_
Can I wait for it?	**¿Puedo esperar?** _pwedo esperar_
Can you repair it today?	**¿Puede arreglarlo hoy?** _pwedeh arreglarlo oy_
When will it be ready?	**¿Cuándo estará listo?** _kwando estara leesto_
How much will it cost?	**¿Cuánto costará?** _kwanto kostara_
That's outrageous!	**¡Eso es un escándalo!** _eso es oon eskandalo_
Can I have a receipt for my insurance?	**¿Pueden darme un recibo para el seguro?** _pweden darmeh oon retheebo para el segooro_

YOU MAY HEAR

El/la ... no funciona.	The ... isn't working.
No tengo las piezas necesarias.	I don't have the necessary parts.
Tendré que mandar a pedir las piezas.	I will have to order the parts.
Sólo puedo repararlo provisionalmente.	I can only repair it temporarily.
Su coche no tiene arreglo.	Your car is beyond repair.
No se puede arreglar/reparar.	It can't be repaired.
Estará listo ...	It will be ready ...
hoy mismo	later today
mañana	tomorrow
dentro de ... días	in ... days

ACCIDENTS

In the event of an accident:

1. put your red warning triangle about 100 meters behind your car;
2. report the accident to the police; don't leave before they arrive;
3. show your driver's license and insurance papers;
4. give your name, address, insurance company to the other party;
5. report the accident to your insurance company;
6. don't make any written statement without advice of a lawyer or automobile club official;
7. note all relevant details of the other party, any independent witnesses, and the accident.

There has been an accident.	**Ha habido un accidente.** *a abeedo oon aktheedenteh*
It's …	**Ha ocurrido …** *a okoorreedo*
on the highway [motorway]	**en la autopista** *en la aootopeesta*
near …	**cerca de …** *therka deh*
Where's the nearest telephone?	**¿Dónde está el teléfono más cercano?** *dondeh esta el telefono mas therkano*
Call …	**Llame a …** *l-yameh a*
the police	**la policía** *la poleetheeya*
an ambulance	**una ambulancia** *oona amboolantheeya*
the fire department [brigade]	**el cuerpo de bomberos** *el kwerpo deh bomberos*
Can you help me, please?	**¿Puede ayudarme, por favor?** *pwedeh ayoodarmeh por fabor*

Injuries

There are people injured.	**Hay gente herida.** *eye khenteh ereeda*
He's seriously injured.	**Está gravemente herido.** *esta grabementeh ereedo*
He's bleeding.	**Está sangrando.** *esta sangrando*
She's unconscious.	**Está inconsciente.** *esta eenkonstheeyenteh*
He can't breathe/move.	**No puede respirar/moverse.** *no pwedeh respeerar/moberseh*

92

Legal matters

What's your insurance company?	**¿Cuál es su compañía de seguros?** *kwal es soo kompañeeya deh segooros*
What's your name and address?	**¿Cuál es su nombre y su dirección?** *kwal es soo nombreh ee soo deerektheeyon*
The car ran into me.	**Chocó conmigo.** *choko konmeego*
She was driving too fast/ too close.	**Conducía demasiado rápido/cerca.** *kondootheeya demaseeyado rapeedo/therka*
I had the right of way.	**Yo tenía derecho de paso.** *yo teneeya derecho deh paso*
I was (only) driving … kmh.	**(Sólo) conducía a … kilómetros por hora.** *(solo) kondootheeya a … keelometros por ora*
I'd like an interpreter.	**Quiero un intérprete.** *keeyero oon eenterpreteh*
I didn't see the sign.	**No vi la señal.** *no bee la señal*
He/She saw it happen.	**Él/Ella lo vio.** *el/el-ya lo beeyo*
The license plate [registration] number was …	**El número de matrícula era …** *el noomero deh matreekoola era*

YOU MAY HEAR

¿Puedo ver su …, por favor?	Can I see your …, please?
carnet/permiso de conducir	driver's license
certificado del seguro	insurance card [certificate]
documento del registro del coche	vehicle registration
¿A qué hora ocurrió?	What time did it happen?
¿Dónde ocurrió?	Where did it happen?
¿Hubo alguien más involucrado?	Was anyone else involved?
¿Hay testigos?	Are there any witnesses?
Se pasó del límite de velocidad.	You were speeding.
Sus faros no funcionan.	Your lights aren't working.
Tendrá que pagar una multa (en el sitio).	You'll have to pay a fine (on the spot).
Tenemos que tomar su declaración en la comisaría.	You have to make a statement at the station.

ASKING DIRECTIONS

Excuse me, please.	**Disculpe, por favor.** *deeskoolpeh por fabor*
How do I get to …?	**¿Cómo se va a …?** *komo seh ba a*
Where is …?	**¿Dónde está …?** *dondeh esta*
Can you show me where I am on the map?	**¿Puede indicarme dónde estoy en el mapa?** *pwedeh eendeekarmeh dondeh estoy en el mapa*
Can you repeat that, please?	**¿Puede repetir eso, por favor?** *pwedeh repeteer eso por fabor*
More slowly, please.	**Más despacio, por favor.** *mas despatheeyo por fabor*
Thanks for your help.	**Gracias por su ayuda.** *gratheeyas por soo ayooda*

Traveling by car

Is this the right road for …?	**¿Es ésta la carretera para …?** *es esta la karretera para*
How far is it to … from here?	**¿A qué distancia está … de aquí?** *a keh deestantheeya esta … deh akee*
Where does this road lead?	**¿Adónde va esta carretera?** *adondeh ba esta karretera*
How do I get onto the highway [motorway]?	**¿Cómo se va a la autopista?** *komo seh ba a la aootopeesta*
What's the next town called?	**¿Cómo se llama el próximo pueblo?** *komo seh l-yama el prokseemo pweblo*
How long does it take by car?	**¿Cuánto tiempo se tarda en coche?** *kwanto teeyempo seh tarda en kocheh*

ON THE STREET

¿A qué distancia está la estación de trenes? *a keh deestantheeya esta la estatheeyon deh trenes* (How far is it to the train station?)

Diez minutos en coche. *deeyeth meenootos en kocheh* (10 minutes by car.)

Gracias. *gratheeyas* (Thank you.)

Location

Está ...	It's ...
todo recto	straight ahead
a la izquierda	on the left
a la derecha	on the right
al otro lado de la calle	on the other side of the street
en la esquina	on the corner
doblando la esquina	around the corner
yendo hacia ...	in the direction of ...
frente a .../detrás de ...	opposite .../behind ...
al lado de .../después de ...	next to .../after ...
Baje por ...	Go down the ...
bocacalle/calle principal	side street/main street
Cruce ...	Cross the ...
plaza/puente	square/bridge
Tome/Coja ...	Take the ...
el tercer desvío a la derecha	third turn to the right
Tuerza a la izquierda.	Turn left.
después del primer semáforo	after the first traffic light
en el segundo cruce	at the second intersection [crossroad]

By car

Está ... de aquí.	It's ... of here.
al norte/sur	north/south
al este/oeste	east/west
Tome/coja la carretera para ...	Take the road for ...
Se ha equivocado de carretera.	You're on the wrong road.
Tendrá que volver a ...	You'll have to go back to ...
Siga las señales para ...	Follow the signs for ...

How far?

Está ...	It's ...
cerca/no está lejos/bastante lejos	close/not far/a long way
a cinco minutos a pie	5 minutes on foot
a diez minutos en coche	10 minutes by car
aproximadamente a cien metros	about 100 meters from
de final de la calle	by the end of the street

ROAD SIGNS

ACCESO SÓLO	access only
CALLE DE SENTIDO ÚNICO	one-way street
CARRETERA CERRADA	road closed
CEDA EL PASO	yield [give way]
DESVÍO	detour [diversion]
ESCUELA/COLEGIO	school
PÓNGASE EN EL CARRIL	stay in lane [get in lane]
PUENTE BAJO	low bridge
RUTA ALTERNATIVA	alternative route
UTILICE LOS FAROS	use headlights

Town plans

aeropuerto	airport
aparcamiento	parking lot [car park]
aseos	restrooms
calle mayor	main [high] street
campo de actividades deportivas	playing field [sports ground]
casco antiguo	old town
cine	movie theater [cinema]
comisaría de policía	police station
correos (oficina de)	post office
edificio público	public building
estación	station
estación de metro	subway [metro] station
estadio	stadium
iglesia	church
oficina de información	information office
parada de autobús	bus stop
parada de taxis	taxi stand [rank]
parque	park
pasaje subterráneo	underpass
paso de peatones	pedestrian crossing
ruta de autobús	bus route
servicios	toilets
teatro	theater
Usted está aquí.	You are here.
zona peatonal	pedestrian zone [precinct]

SIGHTSEEING
TOURIST INFORMATION OFFICE

Tourist information offices are often situated in the town center; look for **Oficina de turismo** and **Información**.

There are numerous local festivals to look for: e.g. **Las Fallas de Valencia** (March), **La Feria de Sevilla** (April), **San Isidro** (Madrid,15 May), **Los Sanfermines de Pamplona** (July), **La Mercè** (Barcelona, 23 September).

Where's the tourist office?	**¿Dónde está la oficina de turismo?** _dondeh esta la ofeetheena deh tooreesmo_
What are the main points of interest?	**¿Cuáles son los sitios de interés?** _kwales son los seeteeyos deh interes_
We're here for …	**Nos quedaremos aquí …** _nos kedaremos akee_
a few hours	**unas horas** _oonas oras_
a day/week	**un día/una semana** _oon deeya/oona semana_
Can you recommend a(n) …?	**¿Puede recomendarme …?** _pwedeh rekomendarmeh_
a sightseeing tour	**un recorrido por los sitios de interés** _oon rekorreedo por los seeteeyos deh eenteres_
an excursion	**una excursión** _oona ekskoorseeyon_
a boat trip	**una excursión en barco** _oona eskoorseeyon en barko_
Are these brochures free?	**¿Son gratis estos folletos?** _son gratees estos fol-yetos_
Do you have any information on …?	**¿Tiene alguna información sobre …?** _teeyeneh algoona eenformatheeyon sobreh_
Are there any trips to …?	**¿Hay excursiones a …?** _eye ekskoorseeyones a_

EXCURSIONS

How much does the tour cost?	**¿Cuánto cuesta la visita?** *kwanto kwesta la beeseeta*
Is lunch included?	**¿Va incluida la comida?** *ba eenklooeeda la komeeda*
Where do we leave from?	**¿De dónde se sale?** *deh dondeh seh saleh*
What time does the tour start?	**¿A qué hora comienza la visita?** *a keh ora komeeyentha la beeseeta*
What time do we get back?	**¿A qué hora volvemos?** *a keh ora bolbemos*
Do we have free time in …?	**¿Tenemos tiempo libre en …?** *tenemos teeyempo leebreh en*
Is there an English-speaking guide?	**¿Hay un guía que hable inglés?** *eye oon geeya keh ableh eengles*

On tour

Are we going to see …?	**¿Vamos a ver …?** *bamos a behr*
We'd like to have a look at …	**Queremos echar un vistazo a …** *keremos echar oon beestatho a*
Can we stop here …?	**¿Podemos parar aquí …?** *podemos parar akee*
to take photographs	**para hacer fotos** *para ather fotos*
to buy souvenirs	**para comprar recuerdos** *para komprar rekwerdos*
for the restrooms [toilets]	**para ir al servicio** *para eer al serbeetheeyo*
Would you take a photo of us, please?	**¿Podría sacarnos una foto, por favor?** *podreeya sakarnos oona foto por fabor*
How long do we have here/in …?	**¿Cuánto tiempo tenemos para estar aquí/en …?** *kwanto teeyempo tenemos para estar akee/en*
Wait! … isn't back yet.	**¡Esperen! … todavía no ha vuelto.** *esperen … todabeeya no a bwelto*
Stop the bus, my child is feeling sick.	**Pare el autobús – mi hijo(-a) se marea.** *pareh el aootoboos mee eekho(-a) se mareya*

SIGHTS

Town maps are on display in city centers, train, tram, and many bus stations, and at tourist information offices. Many tourist offices will give you a free folding map of the town with useful tourist information.

Where is the …	**¿Dónde está …?** _dondeh esta_
abbey	**la abadía** _la abadeeya_
battle site	**el lugar de la batalla** _el loogar deh la batal-ya_
botanical garden	**el jardín botánico** _el khardeen botaneeko_
castle	**el castillo** _el kasteel-yo_
cathedral	**la catedral** _la katedral_
church	**la iglesia** _la eegleseeya_
downtown area	**el centro** _el thentro_
fountain	**la fuente** _la fwenteh_
library	**la biblioteca** _la beebleeyoteka_
market	**el mercado** _el merkado_
(war) memorial	**el monumento (a los caídos)** _el monoomento (a los kaeedos)_
monastery	**el monasterio** _el monastereeyo_
museum	**el museo** _el mooseyo_
old town	**el casco antiguo** _el kasko anteegwo_
opera house	**el teatro de la ópera** _el teyatro deh la opera_
palace	**el palacio** _el palatheeyo_
park	**el parque** _el parkheh_
parliament building	**el palacio de las cortes** _el palatheeyo deh las kortes_
ruins	**las ruinas** _la rooeena_
shopping area	**la zona de tiendas** _la thona deh teeyendas_
theater	**el teatro** _el teyatro_
tower	**la torre** _la torreh_
town hall	**el ayuntamiento** _el ayoontameeyento_
viewpoint	**el mirador** _el meerador_
Can you show me on the map?	**¿Puede indicarme en el mapa?** _pwedeh eendeekarmeh en el mapa_

ADMISSION

Museums are usually closed on Mondays, important holidays, and for the daily siesta (2 p.m. to 4 p.m.). Usual opening hours are 10 a.m.to 1 or 2 p.m. and 4 p.m. to 6 or 7 p.m.

Is the … open to the public?	**¿Está … abierto(-a) al público?** *esta … abeeyerto(-a) al poobleeko*
Can we look around?	**¿Podemos echarle un vistazo a los alrededores?** *podemos echarleh oon beestatho a los alrrededores*
What are the hours?	**¿A qué hora abre?** *a keh ora abreh*
When does it close?	**¿A qué hora cierra?** *a keh ora theeyerra*
Is it open on Sundays?	**¿Está abierto los domingos?** *esta abeeyerto los domeengos*
When's the next guided tour?	**¿Cuándo es la próxima visita con guía?** *kwando es la prokseema beeseeta kon geeya*
Do you have a guide book (in English)?	**¿Tiene una guía (en inglés)?** *teeyeneh oona geeya (en eengles)*
Can I take photos?	**¿Puedo hacer fotos?** *pwedo ather fotos*
Is there access for the disabled?	**¿Tiene acceso para minusválidos?** *teyeneh aktheso para meenoosbaleedos*
Is there an audioguide in English?	**¿Tienen auriculares para seguir la visita en inglés?** *teeyenen aooreekoolares para segeer la beeseeta en eengles*

Paying/Tickets

How much is the entrance fee?	**¿Cuánto cuesta la entrada?** *kwanto kwesta la entrada*
Are there any reductions?	**¿Hacen descuento?** *athen deskwento*
children	**los niños** *los neeños*
groups	**los grupos** *los groopos*
senior citizens	**los pensionistas** *los penseeyoneestas*
students	**los estudiantes** *los estoodeeyantes*
the disabled	**los minusválidos** *los meenoosbaleedos*
One adult and two children, please.	**Un adulto y dos niños, por favor.** *oon adoolto ee dos neeños por fabor*

AT THE TICKET COUNTER

Dos adultos, por favor. *dos ad<u>ool</u>tos por fa<u>bor</u>* (*Two adults, please.*)

Doce euros. <u>dot</u>heh eh-oo<u>ros</u> (*12 euros.*)

Aquí tiene. a<u>kee</u> tee<u>ye</u>neh (*Here you are.*)

YOU MAY SEE

ABIERTO/CERRADO	open/closed
ENTRADA GRATUITA	free admission
HORARIO DE VISITAS	visiting hours
LA PRÓXIMA VISITA ES A LA/LAS …	next tour at …
PROHIBIDA LA ENTRADA	no entry
PROHIBIDO UTILIZAR EL FLASH	no flash photography
TIENDA DE RECUERDOS	gift shop
ÚLTIMA VISTA A LAS 17H	last entry at 5 p.m.

IMPRESSIONS

It's …	**Es …** *es*
amazing/brilliant	**increíble/maravilloso** *eenkray<u>ee</u>bleh/marabeel-<u>yo</u>so*
beautiful	**bonito** *bo<u>nee</u>to*
bizarre/strange	**extraño** *eks<u>tra</u>ño*
boring	**aburrido** *aboo<u>rree</u>do*
interesting	**interesante** *eentere<u>san</u>teh*
magnificent	**magnífico** *mag<u>nee</u>feeko*
romantic	**romántico** *ro<u>man</u>teeko*
stunning/superb	**precioso/espléndido** *prethee<u>o</u>so/es<u>plen</u>deedo*
terrible	**terrible** *te<u>rree</u>bleh*
ugly	**feo** *feyo*
It's a good value.	**Está muy bien de precio.** *es<u>ta</u> mwee bee<u>yen</u> deh <u>pre</u>theeyo*
It's a rip-off.	**Es un timo.** *es oon <u>tee</u>mo*
I like/don't like it.	**Me gusta./No me gusta.** *meh <u>goo</u>sta/no meh <u>goo</u>sta*

TOURIST GLOSSARY

a escala uno:cien scale 1:100

acuarela watercolor

aguja spire

al estilo (de) in the style of

ala wing *(building)*

almena battlement

antigüedades antiques

aposentos apartments *(royal)*

arma weapon

armadura armory

artesanía crafts

baños baths

biblioteca library

boceto sketch

bóveda vault

cementerio churchyard

cenotafio cenotaph

cerámica pottery

conferencia lecture

construido(-a) en ... built in ...

contrafuerte buttress

corona crown

cripta crypt

cuadro painting

cúpula dome

decorado(-a) por ... decorated by ...

descubierto(-a) en ... discovered in ...

destruido(-a) por ... destroyed by ...

detalle detail

dibujo drawing

diseñado(-a) por ... designed by ...

diseño design

donado(-a) por ... donated by ...

dorado(-a) gilded

dorado(-a) gold(en)

edificio building

emperador emperor

emperatriz empress

empezado(-a) en ... started in ...

entrada doorway

eregido(-a) en ... erected in ...

escalera staircase

escenario stage

escuela de school of

escultor sculptor

escultura sculpture

exposición exhibit

exposición exhibition

exposición temporal temporary exhibit

fachada facade

foso moat

friso frieze

fundado(-a) en ... founded in ...

gárgola gargoyle

grabado engraving

grabado etching

jardín de diseño formal formal garden

joyas jewelry

lápida headstone	**primer piso** level 1
lienzo canvas	**puerta** gate
mandado(-a) por ... commissioned by ...	**reconstruido (-a) en ...** rebuilt in ...
mármol marble	**reina** queen
la maqueta model	**reino** reign
moneda coin	**reloj** clock
muebles furniture	**restaurado(-a) en ...** restored in ...
muestra display	**retablo** tableau
murió en ... died in ...	**retrato** portrait
muro *(outside)* wall	**rey** king
nacido(-a) en ... born in ...	**salón para grandes recepciones** stateroom
obra maestra masterpiece	
óleos oils	**siglo** century
pabellón pavilion	**silla del coro** choir (stall)
paisaje landscape painting	**talla** carving
pared *(inside)* wall	**talla de cera** waxwork
patio courtyard	**tapiz** tapestry
piedra stone	**terminado(-a) en ...** completed in ...
piedra semipreciosa gemstone	
pila bautismal font	**torre** tower
pintado(-a) por ... painted by ...	**traje** costume
	tumba grave
pintor/pintora painter	**tumba** tomb
placa plaque	**vestíbulo** foyer
plata silver/silverware	**vidriera** stained-glass window
por ... by ... *(person)*	**vivió** lived
prestado(-a) a ... on loan to ...	

WHAT?/WHEN?

What's that building?	**¿Qué es ese edificio?** *keh es eseh edee<u>fee</u>theeyo*
When was it built/painted?	**¿Cuándo se construyó/pintó?** *<u>kwan</u>do seh konstroo<u>yo</u>/peen<u>to</u>*
What style is that?	**¿De qué estilo es eso?** *deh keh es<u>tee</u>lo es <u>e</u>so*

103

STYLES

realizaciones romanas   200 b.c.–500 a.d.

Ruins of Roman civilization are commonplace in Spain especially the aqueduct at Segovia, the bridge at Córdoba, the triumphal arch in Tarragona, the theatre in Mérida.

arte árabe   ca. 8–end 15

Moorish architecture and art had a huge influence in Spain; especially ornamental brickwork, fretted woodwork, mosaics, calligraphy, carved plaster work. Three great periods can be identified: arte califal (ca. 8–9th, especially the horseshoe-shaped arch of mosque in Córdoba), arte almohade (ca. 10–1250, especially the Giralda tower in Seville), arte granadino (1250–1492, especially the stucco and ceramics in the Alhambra, Granada).

gótico   ca. 13–end 15

Very complex architectural forms, using pointed arches, rib vaults and elaborate stone ornamentation (Isabelline); especially the cathedrals of Burgos, León, Toledo, Seville. This evolved into Plateresque – a lacelike carving of intricate facades; especially the Patio de las Escuelas, Salamanca.

renacimiento   ca. 15–16

The Renaissance left many monuments in Spain; especially El Escorial near Madrid and the palace of Charles V in the Alhambra.

barroco   ca. 17–18

Exuberant architectural style, especially the convent of San Esteban in Salamanca and the Palacio del Marqués de Dos Aguas in Valencia.

siglo de Oro   ca.17

The Golden Century saw a flourishing of the arts; especially the artists El Greco, Velázquez, Zurbarán, and Murillo; and the writers Miguel de Cervantes, Fray Luis de León, and Santa Teresa.

modernismo   ca. late 19–20

A period of crisis in national self-confidence saw world-renowned cultural figures; especially the artists Picasso, Miró, and Dalí; the architect Gaudí; and the writers Unamuno and Lorca.

RULERS

romana   206 b.c.–410 a.d.

The Romans occupied Spain on defeating the Carthaginians in the Second Punic War. 600 years of rule brought a road network, seaports and skills in mining, agriculture and trade. On the collapse of the Roman Empire, Spain was invaded and dominated by the Visigoths.

árabe 711–1492
The first Moorish invasion from North Africa defeated the Visigoths. For almost 800 years Moorish control of Spain fluctuated as the Christian Reconquest expanded. Ferdinand and Isabella completed their expulsion in 1492.

reyes católicos 1474–1516
National unity under Isabel of Castile and Fernando of Aragón saw the Spanish Inquisition (**Inquisición**) set up in 1478 and Columbus claim newly discovered lands for Spain (1492).

la casa de Asturias 1516–1700
The Habsburg House, financed by plundered wealth from the New World, extended its influence: Charles V (**Carlos I**) made claims on Burgundy, the Netherlands, and Italy.

los Borbones 1700–1923
A period of continued military and cultural decline under the Bourbons. The invasion by Napoleon in 1808 forced the abdication of Carlos IV. The 19th century saw the loss of most of Spain's territories in Central and South America.

dictadura del General Franco 1939–75
In the bloody Spanish Civil War (**guerra civil Española**) General Franco's fascist forces overthrow the Republic and declare a dictatorship that lasts until his death.

la democracia 1975–
Juan Carlos I becomes a constitutional monarch. 1992 saw EXPO '92 in Seville, the Olympics in Barcelona, and Madrid nominated the Cultural Capital of Europe.

RELIGION

Predominantly Roman Catholic, Spain is rich in cathedrals and churches. Most large churches are open to the public during the day, services should be respected. Cover bare shoulders before entering.

Catholic/Protestant church	**la Iglesia católica/protestante** *la eegleseeya katoleeka/protestanteh*
mosque/synagogue	**la mezquita/la sinagoga** *la methkeeta/la seenagoga*
mass/the service	**la misa/el servicio** *la meesa/el serveetheeyo*

IN THE COUNTRYSIDE

I'd like a map of … **Quiero un mapa de …**
keeyero oon mapa deh

this region **esta región** *esta rekheeyon*

walking routes **las rutas de senderismo**
las rootas deh sendereesmo

bicycle routes **las rutas para bicicletas**
las rootas para beetheekletas

How far is it to …? **¿A qué distancia está …?**
a keh deestantheeya esta

Is there a right of way? **¿Hay derecho de paso?**
eye derecho deh paso

Is there a route **¿Hay una carretera a …?**
to …? *eye oona karretera a*

Can you show me **¿Puede indicármelo en el mapa?**
on the map? *pwedeh eendeekarmelo en el mapa*

I'm lost. **Me he perdido.** *meh eh perdeedo*

Organized walks/hikes

When does the guided **¿Cuándo empieza el paseo/la excursión a**
walk/hike start? **pie?** *kwando empeeyetha el paseyo/*
la ekskoorseeyon a peeyeh

When will we return? **¿Cuándo volveremos?** *kwando bolberemos*

What is the walk/hike like? **¿Cómo es el paseo/la excursión a pie?**
komo es el paseyo/la ekskoorseeyon a peeyeh

gentle/medium/tough **fácil/regular/duro** *fatheel/regoolar/dooro*

Where do we meet? **¿Dónde nos encontramos?**
dondeh nos enkontramos

I'm exhausted. **Estoy exhausto(-a).** *estoy eksawsto(-a)*

How high is that mountain? **¿Qué altura tiene esa montaña?**
keh altoora teeyeneh esa montaña

What kind of … is that? **¿Qué clase de … es ése(-a)?**
keh klaseh deh … es ese(-a)

animal/bird **animal/pájaro** *aneemal/pakharo*

flower/tree **flor/árbol** *flor/arbol*

Geographical features

bridge	**el puente**	*el pwenteh*
cave	**la cueva**	*la kweba*
cliff	**el acantilado**	*el akanteelado*
farm	**la granja**	*la grankha*
field	**el campo**	*el kampo*
footpath	**el sendero**	*el sendero*
forest	**el bosque**	*el boskeh*
hill	**la colina**	*la koleena*
lake	**el lago**	*el lago*
mountain	**la montaña**	*la montaña*
mountain pass	**el paso de montaña**	*el paso deh montaña*
mountain range	**la cordillera**	*la kordeel-yera*
nature reserve	**la reserva natural**	*la reserba natooral*
panorama	**el panorama**	*el panorama*
park	**el parque**	*el parkeh*
pass	**el paso**	*el paso*
path	**el camino**	*el kameeno*
peak	**el pico**	*el peeko*
picnic area	**la zona para picnics**	*la thona para peekneeks*
pond	**el estanque**	*el estankeh*
rapids	**los rápidos**	*los rapeedos*
ravine	**el barranco**	*el barranko*
river	**el río**	*el reeyo*
sea	**el mar**	*el mar*
spa (place to stay)	**el balneario**	*el balneareeyo*
stream	**el arroyo**	*el arroyo*
valley	**el valle**	*el bal-yeh*
viewing point	**el mirador**	*el meerador*
village	**el pueblo**	*el pweblo*
vineyard/winery	**el viñedo**	*el beeñedo*
waterfall	**la catarata**	*la katarata*
wood	**el bosque**	*el boskeh*

LEISURE

EVENTS

Local papers and, in large cities, weekly entertainment guides (such as **Guía del Ocio**) will tell you what's on.

Tickets for concerts, theater, and other cultural events are on sale at special ticket agencies. In small towns these may be in kiosks, book or music stores: ask at the local tourist office.

Do you have a program of events?	**¿Tiene un programa de espectáculos?** *teeyeneh oon programa deh espektakoolos*
Can you recommend a ...?	**¿Puede recomendarme un(a) ...?** *pwedeh rekomendarmeh oon(a)*
Is there a ... somewhere?	**¿Hay ... en algún sitio?** *eye ... en algoon seeteeyo*
ballet/concert	**un ballet/un concierto** *oon bal-yet/oon kontheeyerto*
movie [film]	**una película** *oona peleekoola*
opera	**una ópera** *oona opera*
When does it start?	**¿A qué hora empieza?** *a keh ora empeeyetha*
When does it end?	**¿A qué hora termina?** *a keh ora termeena*

Availability

Where can I get tickets?	**¿Dónde se pueden comprar las entradas?** *dondeh seh pweden komprar las entradas*
Are there any seats for tonight?	**¿Hay entradas para esta noche?** *eye entradas para esta nocheh*
I'm sorry, we're sold out.	**Lo siento, no quedan entradas.** *lo seeyento no kedan entradas*
There are ... of us.	**Somos ...** *somos*

Tickets

How much are the seats?	**¿Cuánto cuestan estas localidades?** _kwanto kwestan las lokaleedades_
Do you have anything cheaper?	**¿Tiene algo más barato?** _teeyeneh algo mas barato_
I'd like to reserve …	**Quiero reservar …** _keeyero reserbar_
three for Sunday evening	**tres para el domingo por la noche** _tres para el domeengo por la nocheh_
one for the Friday matinée	**una para la matiné del viernes** _oona para la mateeneh del beeyernes_
May I have a program, please?	**¿Puede darme un programa, por favor?** _pwedeh darmeh oon programa por fabor_
Where's the coatcheck [cloakroom]?	**¿Dónde está el guardarropa?** _dondeh esta el gwardarropa_
Where's the water fountain?	**¿Dónde está el bebedero?** _dondeh esta el bebehdero_

ESSENTIAL

¿Cuál es … de su tarjeta de crédito?	What's your credit card …?
el número	number
la fecha de caducidad	expiration [expiry] date
Por favor, recoja las entradas …	Please pick up the tickets …
antes de las … de la tarde	by … p.m.
en el mostrador de reservas	at the reservation desk

AT THE BOX OFFICE

¿Tiene un programa de espectáculos? _teeyeneh oon programa de espektakoolos_ (Do you have a program of events?)

Por supuesto. _por soopwesto_ (Of course.)

Gracias. _gratheeyas_ (Thank you.)

MOVIES [CINEMA]

Foreign films are usually dubbed into Spanish, but some movie theaters show films in the original version (**v.o.**).

Spain has a developing film industry of its own, with world-famous directors such as Almodóvar and Buñuel.

Is there a movie theater [multiplex cinema] near here?	**¿Hay un multicine cerca de aquí?** *eye oon moolteetheeneh therka deh akee*
What's playing at the movies [on at the cinema] tonight?	**¿Qué ponen en el cine esta noche?** *keh ponen en el theneh esta nocheh*
Is the film dubbed/subtitled?	**¿Está doblada/subtitulada la película?** *esta doblada/soobteetoolada la peleekoola*
Is the film in the original English?	**¿Está la película en el inglés original?** *esta la peleekoola en el eengles oreekheenal*
Who's the main actor/actress?	**¿Quién es el actor/la actriz principal?** *keeyen es el aktor/la aktreeth preentheepal*
A ..., please.	**..., por favor** *... por fabor*
box [carton] of popcorn	**un cucurucho de palomitas** *oon kookooroocho deh palomeetas*
chocolate ice cream	**un helado de chocolate** *oon elado deh chokolateh*
hot dog	**un perrito caliente** *oon perreeto kaleeyenteh*
soft drink	**un refresco** *oon refresko*
small/regular/large	**pequeño/de tamaño normal/grande** *pekeño/deh tamaño normal/grandeh*

THEATER

What's playing at the ...theater?	**¿Qué función ponen en el teatro ...?** *keh foontheeyon ponen en el teyatro*
Who's the playwright?	**¿Quién es el autor?** *keeyen es el aootor*
Do you think I'd enjoy it?	**¿Cree que me gustará?** *kreyeh keh meh goostara*
I don't know much Spanish.	**No sé mucho español.** *no seh moocho español*

OPERA/BALLET/DANCE

Who's the composer/soloist?	**¿Quién es el/la compositor(a)/solista?** _keeyen es el/la komposeetor(a)/soleesta_
Is formal dress required?	**¿Hay que vestirse de etiqueta?** _eye keh besteerseh deh eteeketa_
Where's the opera house?	**¿Dónde está el teatro de la ópera?** _dondeh esta el teyatro deh la opera_
Who's dancing?	**¿Quién baila?** _keeyen bayla_
I'm interested in contemporary dance.	**Me interesa la danza contemporánea.** _meh eenteresa la dantha kontemporaneya_

MUSIC/CONCERTS

Where's the concert hall?	**¿Dónde está la sala de conciertos?** _dondeh esta la sala deh kontheeyertos_
Which orchestra/band is playing?	**¿Qué orquesta/grupo toca?** _keh orkesta/groopo toka_
What are they playing?	**¿Qué van a tocar?** _keh ban a tokar_
Who's the conductor/soloist?	**¿Quién es el/la director(a)/solista?** _keeyen es el/la deerektor(a)/soleesta_
Who's the support band?	**¿Quiénes son los teloneros?** _keeyenes son los teloneros_
I really like …	**Me gusta mucho …** _meh goosta moocho_
country music	**la música country** _la mooseeka kaoontree_
folk music	**la música folk** _la mooseeka folk_
jazz	**el jazz** _el jazz_
music of the sixties	**la música de los sesentas** _la mooseeka deh los sesentas_
pop	**la música pop** _la mooseeka pop_
rock music	**la música rock** _la mooseeka rok_
soul music	**la música soul** _la mooseeka sowl_
Have you ever heard of her/him?	**¿Ha oído hablar de ella/él?** _a oyeedo ablar deh el-ya/el_
Are they popular?	**¿Son famosos?** _son famosos_

111

NIGHTLIFE

What is there to do in the evenings?	**¿Qué se puede hacer por las noches?** *keh seh pwedeh ather por las noches*
Can you recommend a good …?	**¿Puede recomendarme un buen …?** *pwedeh rekomendarmeh oon bwen*
Is there a … in town?	**¿Hay … en esta ciudad?** *eye … en esta theeyoodath*
bar	**un bar** *oon bar*
casino	**un casino** *oon kaseeno*
discotheque	**una discoteca** *oona deeskoteka*
gay club	**un club gay** *oon kloob gay*
nightclub	**un club nocturno** *oon kloob noktoorno*
restaurant	**un restaurante** *oon restawranteh*
Is there a floor show/cabaret?	**¿Hay un espectáculo de cabaret?** *eye oon espektakoolo deh kabaret*
What type of music do they play?	**¿Qué tipo de música tocan?** *keh teepo deh mooseeka tokan*
How do I get there?	**¿Cómo se va allí?** *komo seh ba al-yee*

Admission

What time does the show start?	**¿A qué hora empieza el espectáculo?** *a keh ora empeeyetha el espektakoolo*
Is evening dress required?	**¿Hay que ir con traje de noche?** *eye keh eer kon trakheh deh nocheh*
Is there a cover charge?	**¿Hay un precio de entrada?** *eye oon pretheeyo deh entradah*
Is a reservation necessary?	**¿Hay que hacer una reserva?** *eye keh ather oona reserba*
Do we need to be members?	**¿Hay que ser socios?** *eye keh sehr sotheeyos*
How long will we have to stand in line [queue]?	**¿Cuánto tiempo tendremos que hacer cola?** *kwanto teeyempo tendremos keh ather kola*

YOU MAY SEE

INCLUYE UNA CONSUMICIÓN GRATIS	includes one complimentary drink

CHILDREN

Can you recommend something for the children?
¿**Puede recomendarme algo para los niños?** _pwedeh rekomendarmeh algo para los neeños_

Are there changing facilities here for babies?
¿**Tienen instalaciones para cambiar al bebé?** _teeyenen eenstalatheeyones para kambeeyar al bebeh_

Where are the restrooms [toilets]?
¿**Dónde están los servicios?** _dondeh estan los serveetheeyos_

amusement arcade
el salón recreativo _el salon rekreateebo_

fairground
la feria _la fereeya_

kiddie [paddling] pool
la piscina infantil _la peestheena eenfanteel_

playground
el patio de juegos _el pateeyo deh khwegos_

play group
el club infantil _el kloob eefanteel_

zoo
el zoológico _el thoo-o-lokheeko_

Babysitting

Can you recommend a reliable babysitter?
¿**Puede recomendarme una canguro de confianza?** _pwedeh rekomendarmeh oona kangooro deh konfeeyantha_

Is there constant supervision?
¿**Supervisan a los niños constantemente?** _sooperbeesan a los neeños konstantementeh_

Is the staff properly trained?
¿**Están cualificados los empleados?** _estan kwaleefeekados los empleados_

When can I bring them?
¿**Cuándo puedo dejarlos?** _kwando pwedo dekharlos_

I'll pick them up at …
Los recogeré a las … _los rekokhereh a las_

We'll be back by …
Volveremos antes de las … _bolberemos antes deh las_

She's 3 and he's 18 months.
La niña tiene tres años y el niño dieciocho meses. _la neeña teeyeneh tres años ee el neeño deeyetheeocho meses_

SPORTS

Whether you are a fan or a participant, Spain has the weather and facilities to satisfy most sports enthusiasts. Soccer [football] (**fútbol**) is the most popular sport, inspiring fierce devotion – particularly in Madrid and Barcelona. Spain is famous for its golf courses, especially on the Costa del Sol. Tennis, horseback riding, and hill climbing are also popular. And look for **pelota** (**jai alai** in the Basque country and Latin America) – a furiously fast ball game involving curved wicker-basket gloves.

Spectator Sports

Is there a soccer [football] game [match] this Saturday?	**¿Hay un partido de fútbol este sábado?** *eye oon parteedo deh footbol esteh sabado*
Which teams are playing?	**¿Qué equipos juegan?** *keh ekeepos khwegan*
Can you get me a ticket?	**¿Puede conseguirme una entrada?** *pwedeh konsegeermeh oona entrada*
What's the admission charge?	**¿Cuánto cobran por entrar?** *kwanto kobran por entrar*
Where's the racetrack [racecourse]?	**¿Dónde está el hipódromo?** *dondeh esta el eepodromo*
Where can I place a bet?	**¿Dónde puedo hacer una apuesta?** *dondeh pwedo ather oona apwesta*
What are the odds on ...?	**¿A cómo están las apuestas para ...?** *a komo estan las apwestas para*

athletics	**atletismo** *atleteesmo*
basketball	**baloncesto** *balonthesto*
cycling	**ciclismo** *theekleesmo*
golf	**golf** *golf*
horseracing	**carreras de caballos** *karreras deh kabal-yos*
soccer [football]	**fútbol** *footbol*
swimming	**natación** *natatheeyon*
tennis	**tenis** *tenees*
volleyball	**voleybol** *boleebol*

Participating

Where's the nearest …?	**¿Dónde está … más cercano?** _dondeh esta … mas therkano_
golf course	**el campo de golf** _el kampo deh golf_
sports club	**el polideportivo** _el poleedeporteebo_
Where are the tennis courts?	**¿Dónde están las pistas de tenis?** _dondeh estan las peestas deh tenees_
What's the charge per …?	**¿Cuánto cuesta por …?** _kwanto kwesta por_
day/hour	**día/hora** _deeya/ora_
game/round	**partido/juego** _parteedo/khwego_
Do I need to be a member?	**¿Hay que ser socio?** _eye keh sehr sotheeyo_
Where can I rent …?	**¿Dónde puedo alquilar …?** _dondeh pwedo alkeelar_
boots	**unas botas** _oonas botas_
clubs	**unos palos de golf** _oonos palos deh golf_
equipment	**el equipo** _el ekeepo_
a racket	**una raqueta** _oona raketa_
Can I get lessons?	**¿Me pueden dar clases?** _meh pweden dar klases_
Is there an aerobics class?	**¿Hay clases de aerobic?** _eye klases deh ayrobeek_
Do you have a fitness room?	**¿Tienen un gimnasio?** _teeyenen oon khimnaseeyo_

YOU MAY SEE

PROHIBIDO PESCAR	no fishing
SÓLO PARA LOS TENEDORES DE LICENCIA	permit holders only
VESTUARIOS	changing rooms

YOU MAY HEAR

Lo siento, no quedan plazas.	I'm sorry, we're booked.
Hay que pagar depósito de …	There's a deposit of …
¿Qué talla tiene?	What size are you?
Necesita una foto tamaño carnet.	You need a passport-size photo.

At the beach

Spain offers hundreds of miles of beaches for every taste. The most developed offer a full range of facilities for water sports; nor is it too difficult to locate near-deserted coves for a quieter time.

Is the beach …?	**¿Es la playa …?** es la _playa_
pebbly/sandy	**de guijarros/de arena** deh gee_kha_rros/deh a_re_na
Is there a … here?	**¿Hay … aquí?** eye … a_kee_
children's pool	**una piscina para niños** _oo_na pees_thee_na _para nee_ños
swimming pool	**una piscina** _oo_na pees_thee_na
indoor/outdoor	**cubierta/al aire libre** koobee_yer_ta/al _ay_reh _lee_breh
Is it safe to swim/dive here?	**¿Es seguro nadar/tirarse de cabeza aquí?** es se_goo_ro na_dar/teerar_se deh ka_be_tha a_kee_
Is it safe for children?	**¿Es seguro(-a) para los niños?** es se_goo_ro(-a) _para_ los _nee_ños
Is there a lifeguard?	**¿Hay socorrista?** eye soko_rree_sta
I want to rent …	**Quiero alquilar …** kee_ye_ro alkee_lar_
deck chair	**una tumbona** _oo_na toom_bo_na
jet ski	**una moto acuática** _oo_na _mo_to a_kwa_teeka
motorboat	**una motora** _oo_na mo_to_ra
rowboat	**una barca de remos** _oo_na _bar_ka deh _re_mos
sailboat	**un velero** oon be_le_ro
diving equipment	**un equipo de buceo** oon e_kee_po deh boo_tha_yo
umbrella [sunshade]	**una sombrilla** _oo_na som_breel_-ya
surfboard	**una tabla de surf** _oo_na _ta_bla deh soorf
water skis	**unos esquís acuáticos** _oo_nos es_kees_ a_kwa_teekos
windsurfer	**una tabla de windsurf** _oo_na _ta_bla deh _ween_soorf
For … hours.	**Por … horas.** por … _o_ras

Skiing

Spain's 27 ski resorts attract an increasing number of devotees. Most are situated in the Pyrenees (e.g. **Baqueira-Beret, La Molina, Pas de la Casa, Cerler**), while the Andalusian **Sierra Nevada** offers Europe's sunniest skiing.

I'd like to rent …	**Quiero alquilar …** *keeyero alkeelar*
poles	**unos bastones** *oonos bastones*
skates	**unos patines** *oonos pateenes*
ski boots/skis	**unas botas de esquiar/unos esquís** *oonas botas deh eskeeyar/oonos eskees*
These are too …	**Estos(-as) son demasiado …** *estos(as) son demaseeyado*
big/small	**grandes/pequeños** *grandes/pekeños*
These are too loose/tight.	**Están demasiado sueltos/apretados.** *estan demaseeyado sweltos/apretados*
A lift pass for a day/ five days, please.	**Un pase de teleférico para un día/cinco días, por favor.** *oon paseh deh telefereeko para oon deeya/theenko deeyas por fabor*
I'd like to join the ski school.	**Quiero tomar clases de esquí.** *keeyero dar klases deh eskee*
I'm a beginner.	**Soy principiante.** *soy preentheepeeyanteh*
I'm experienced.	**Tengo experiencia.** *tengo espereeyen theeya*

YOU MAY SEE

ARRASTRE	drag lift
TELEFÉRICO/CABINA	cable car/gondola
TELESILLA	chair lift

Bullfight

The bullfight (**la corrida**) may fascinate or appall you. First the matador goads the bull with a large cape. Then the **picador** weakens the bull by lancing its neck. **Banderilleros** on foot thrust three barbed sticks between its shoulder blades. The matador returns to taunt the bull with a small red cape, leading up to the final climax of the kill. The bullfighting season lasts from March to October.

I'd like to see a bullfight.	**Quiero ver una corrida.** *keeyero behr oona korreeda*

MAKING FRIENDS

INTRODUCTIONS

Greetings vary according to how well you know someone. The following is a guide. It's polite to shake hands, both when you meet and say good-bye; it is considered impolite not to.

Begin any conversation, whether with a friend, shop assistant or policeman, with a "**buenos días.**" Speak to them using the formal form of "you" (**usted**) until you are asked to use the familiar form (**tú**).

In Spanish, there are three forms for "you" (taking different verb forms): **tú** (singular) and **vosotros** (plural) are used when talking to relatives, close friends and children (and between young people); **usted** (singular) and **ustedes** (plural) – often abbreviated to **Ud./Uds**. – are used in all other cases. If in doubt, use **usted/ustedes**.

Hello, I don't think we've met.	**Hola, no nos conocemos.** _ola no nos kono<u>the</u>mos_
My name is …	**Me llamo …** _meh l-<u>ya</u>mo_
May I introduce …?	**Quiero presentarle a …** _kee<u>ye</u>ro presen<u>tar</u>leh a_
John, this is …	**John, éste(-a) es …** _jon <u>es</u>teh(-a) es_
Pleased to meet you.	**Encantado(-a) de conocerle(-la).** _enkan<u>ta</u>do(-a) deh kono<u>ther</u>le(-la)_
What's your name?	**¿Cómo se llama?** _<u>ko</u>mo seh l-<u>ya</u>ma_
How are you?	**¿Cómo está?** _<u>ko</u>mo es<u>ta</u>_
Fine, thanks. And you?	**Bien, gracias. ¿Y usted?** _bee<u>ye</u>n <u>gra</u>theeyas. ee oos<u>te</u>th_

AT A RECEPTION

Me llamo Sheryl. _meh l-<u>ya</u>mo sheryl_ (My name is Sheryl.)

Mucho gusto. Me llamo José. _<u>moo</u>cho <u>goo</u>stoh meh l-<u>ya</u>mo ho<u>seh</u>_ (My pleasure. My name is José.)

El gusto es mío. _el <u>goo</u>stoh es <u>mee</u>oh_ (The pleasure is mine.)

Where are you from?

Where are you from?	**¿De dónde es usted?** *deh dondeh es oosteth*
Where were you born?	**¿Dónde nació?** *dondeh natheeyo*
I'm from …	**Soy de …** *soy deh*
Australia	**Australia** *awoostraleeya*
Britain	**Gran Bretaña** *gran bretaña*
Canada	**Canadá** *kanada*
England	**Inglaterra** *eenglaterra*
Ireland	**Irlanda** *eerlanda*
Scotland	**Escocia** *eskotheeya*
the U.S.	**Estados Unidos** *estados ooneedos*
Wales	**Gales** *gales*
Where do you live?	**¿Dónde vive?** *dondeh beebeh*
What part of ,,, are you from?	**¿De qué parte de … es usted?** *deh keh parteh deh … es oosteth*
Spain	**España** *españa*
Argentina	**Argentina** *arkhenteena*
México	**Méjico** *mekheeko*
We come here every year.	**Venimos todos los años.** *beneemos todos los años*
It's my/our first visit.	**Es mi/nuestra primera visita.** *es mee/nwestra preemera beeseeta*
Have you ever been …?	**¿Ha estado alguna vez …?** *a estado algoona beth*
to the U.K./the U.S.	**en Gran Bretaña/Estados Unidos** *en gran bretaña/estados ooneedos*
Do you like it here?	**¿Le gusta esto?** *leh goosta esto*
What do you think of the …?	**¿Qué le parece …?** *keh le paretheh*
food/people	**la cocina/la gente** *la kotheena/la khenteh*
I love the … here.	**Me encanta … de aquí.** *meh enkanta … deh akee*
I don't really like the … here.	**No me gusta demasiado … de aquí.** *no meh goosta demaseeyado … deh akee*

Who are you with?

Who are you with?	**¿Con quién ha venido?** *kon keeyen a beneedo*
I'm on my own.	**He venido solo(-a).** *eh beneedo solo(-a)*
I'm with a friend.	**He venido con un(a) amigo(-a).** *eh beneedo kon oon(a) ameego(-a)*
I'm with my ...	**He venido con ...** *eh beneedo kon*
wife	**mi mujer** *mee mookher*
husband	**mi marido** *mee mareedo*
family	**mi familia** *mee fameeleeya*
children	**mis hijos** *mees eekhos*
parents	**mis padres** *mees padres*
boyfriend/girlfriend	**mi novio(-a)** *mee nobeeyo(-a)*
my father/mother	**mi padre/mi madre** *mee padreh/mee madreh*
my son/daughter	**mi hijo/mi hija** *mee eekho/mee eekha*
my brother/sister	**mi hermano/mi hermana** *mee ermano/mee ermana*
my uncle/aunt	**mi tío/mi tía** *mee teeyo/mee teeya*
Are you married?	**¿Está casado(-a)?** *esta kasado(-a)*
I'm ...	**Estoy ...** *estoy*
married/single	**casado(-a)/soltero(-a)** *kasado(-a)/soltero(-a)*
divorced/separated	**divorciado(-a)/separado(-a)** *deebortheeyado(-a)/separado(-a)*
engaged	**prometido(-a)** *prometeedo*
We live together.	**Vivimos juntos.** *beebeemos khoontos*
Do you have any children?	**¿Tiene hijos?** *teeyeneh eekhos*
We have two boys and a girl.	**Tenemos dos niños y una niña.** *tenemos dos neeños ee oona neeña*
How old are they?	**¿Qué edad tienen?** *keh edath teeyenen*
They're ten and twelve.	**Tienen diez y doce años respectivamente.** *teeyenen deeyeth ee dotheh años respekteebamenteh*

What do you do?

What do you do?	**¿A qué se dedica?** *a keh seh dedeeka*
What are you studying?	**¿Qué estudia?** *keh estoodeeya*
I'm studying …	**Estudio …** *estoodeeyo*
I'm in …	**Me dedico a …** *meh dedeeko a*
business	**asuntos comerciales** *asoontos komertheeyales*
sales	**las ventas** *las bentas*
I'm in engineering.	**Trabajo de ingeniero.** *trabakho deh eenkhenyero*
Who do you work for?	**¿Para quién trabaja?** *para keeyen trabakha*
I work for …	**Trabajo para …** *trabakho para*
I'm a(n) …	**Soy …** *soy*
accountant	**contable** *kontableh*
housewife	**ama de casa** *ama deh kasa*
student	**estudiante** *estoodeeyanteh*
I'm …	**Estoy …** *estoy*
retired	**jubilado(-a)** *khoobeelado(-a)*
between jobs	**entre un trabajo y otro** *entreh oon trabakho ee otro*
I'm self-employed.	**Trabajo por mi cuenta.** *trabakho por mee kwenta*
What are your interests/ hobbies?	**¿Cuáles son sus pasatiempos/hobbies?** *kwales son soos pasateeyempos/hobees*
I like …	**Me gusta(n) …** *me goosta(n)*
music	**la música** *la mooseeka*
reading	**leer** *leh-er*
sports	**los deportes** *los deportes*
I play …	**Juego a …** *khwego a*
Would you like to play …?	**¿Le gustaría jugar a …?** *leh goostareea khoogar a*
cards	**las cartas** *las kartas*
chess	**al ajedrez** *al akhedreth*

121

What weather!

What a lovely day!	**¡Qué día tan bonito!** *keh deeya tan boneeto*
What terrible weather!	**¡Qué tiempo más feo!** *keh teeyempo mas feyo*
Isn't it cold/hot today!	**¡Vaya frío/calor que hace hoy!** *baya freeyo/kalor keh atheh oy*
Is it usually this warm?	**¿Hace normalmente tanto calor como ahora?** *atheh normalmenteh tanto kalor komo a-ora*
Do you think it's going to … tomorrow?	**¿Cree usted que mañana va a …?** *kreyeh oosteth keh mañana ba a*
be a nice day	**hacer buen tiempo** *ather bwen teeyempo*
rain	**llover** *l-yobehr*
snow	**nevar** *nebar*
What's the weather forecast?	**¿Cuál es el pronóstico del tiempo?** *kwal es el pronosteeko del teeyempo*
It's …	**Está …** *esta*
cloudy	**nublado** *nooblado*
rainy	**lluvioso** *l-yoobeeyoso*
stormy	**tronando** *tronando*
It's foggy.	**Hay niebla.** *eye neeyebla*
It's frosty.	**Hay heladas.** *eye eladas*
It's icy.	**Hay hielo.** *eye eeyelo*
It's snowy.	**Hay nieve.** *eye neeyebeh*
It's windy.	**Hace viento.** *atheh beeyento*
Has the weather been like this for long?	**¿Lleva mucho así el tiempo?** *l-yeba moocho asee el teeyempo*
What's the pollen count?	**¿Cuál es el índice de polen?** *kwal es el eendeeteh deh polen*
high/medium/low	**alto/regular/bajo** *alto/regoolar/bakho*

Enjoying your trip?

I'm here on …	**Estoy aquí …** *estoy akee*
business	**en viaje de negocios** *en beeyakheh deh negotheeyos*
vacation [holiday]	**de vacaciones** *deh bakatheeyones*
We came by …	**Vinimos en …** *beeneemos en*
train/bus/plane	**tren/autobús/avión** *tren/aootoboos/abeeyon*
car/ferry	**coche/ferry** *kocheh/ferree*
I have a rental car.	**He alquilado un coche.** *eh alkeelado oon kocheh*
We're staying in/at …	**Nos alojamos en …** *nos alokhamos en*
an apartment	**un apartamento** *oon apartamento*
a hotel/campsite	**un hotel/un cámping** *oon otel/oon kampeen*
with friends	**con unos amigos** *kon oonos ameegos*
Can you suggest …?	**¿Puede sugerirme …?** *pwedeh sookhereermeh*
things to do	**algo que hacer** *algo keh ather*
places to eat/visit	**algunos sitios para comer/ver** *algoonos seeteeyos para komer/behr*
We're having a great/ terrible time.	**Lo estamos pasando muy bien/mal.** *lo estamos pasando mwee beeyen/mal*

YOU MAY HEAR

¿Está de vacaciones?	Are you on vacation?
¿Cómo ha venido aquí?	How did you get here?
¿Qué tal el viaje?	How was the trip?
¿Dónde se aloja?	Where are you staying?
¿Cuánto tiempo lleva aquí?	How long have you been here?
¿Cuánto tiempo va a quedarse?	How long are you staying?
¿Qué ha hecho hasta ahora?	What have you done so far?
¿Qué es lo próximo que va a hacer?	Where are you going next?
¿Está pasando unas buenas vacaciones?	Are you enjoying your vacation?

INVITATIONS

Would you like to have dinner with us on …?
¿Le gustaría cenar con nosotros el …?
leh goostareea thenar kon nosotros el

Are you free for lunch?
¿Puedo invitarle(-la) a comer?
pwedo eenbeetarle(-la) a komer

Can you come for a drink this evening?
¿Puede venir a tomar algo esta noche?
pwede beneer a tomar algo esta nocheh

We are having a party. Can you come?
Vamos a dar una fiesta. ¿Puede venir?
bamos a dar oona feeyesta. pwede beneer

May we join you?
¿Podemos ir con ustedes?
podemos eer kon oostedes

Would you like to join us?
¿Le gustaría venir con nosotros?
leh goostareea beneer kon nosotros

Going out

What are your plans for …?
¿Qué planes tiene(n) para …?
ke planes teeyeneh(n) para

today/tonight
hoy/esta noche *oy/esta nocheh*

tomorrow
mañana *mañana*

Are you free this evening?
¿Está libre esta noche?
esta leebreh esta nocheh

Would you like to …?
¿Le gustaría …? *leh goostareea*

go dancing
ir a bailar *eer a baylar*

go for a drink/meal
ir a tomar una copa/a cenar
eer a tomar oona kopa/a thenar

go for a walk
dar un paseo *dar oon paseyo*

go shopping
ir de compras *eer deh kompras*

Where would you like to go?
¿Adónde le gustaría ir?
adondeh leh goostareeya eer

I'd like to go to …
Me gustaría ir a …
meh goostareea eer a

I'd like to see …
Me gustaría ver … *meh goostareea behr*

Do you enjoy …?
¿Le gusta …? *leh goosta*

Accepting/Declining

Great. I'd love to.	**Estupendo. Me encantaría.**
	estoopendo. meh enkantareeya
Thank you, but I'm busy.	**Gracias, pero estoy ocupado(-a)**
	gratheeyas pero estoy okoopado(-a)
May I bring a friend?	**¿Puedo llevar a un amigo?**
	pwedo l-yebar a oon ameego
Where shall we meet?	**¿Dónde quedamos?** *dondeh kedamos*
I'll meet you …	**Quedamos …** *kedamos*
in the bar	**en el bar** *en el bar*
in front of your hotel	**en frente de su hotel**
	en frenteh deh soo otel
I'll come by [call for you] at 8.	**Pasaré a recogerle a las ocho.**
	pasare a rrekokherle a las ocho
Could we make it a bit earlier/later?	**¿Podríamos quedar un poco antes/ más tarde?** *podreeyamos kedar oon poko antes/mas tardeh*
How about another day?	**¿Qué le parece otro día?**
	keh leh paretheh otro deeya
That will be fine.	**Muy bien.** *mwee beeyen*

Dining out/in

If you are invited home for a meal, always take a gift – a bottle of wine, sparkling wine, chocolates, flowers, for example.

Let me buy you a drink.	**Permítame que le/la invite a una copa.**
	permeetameh keh leh/la eenbeeteh a oona kopa
What are you going to have?	**¿Qué va a tomar?** *keh ba a tomar*
That was a lovely meal.	**Fue una comida estupenda.**
	fweh oona komeeda estoopenda

IN A BAR

¿Le gustaría ir a bailar? *leh goostareea eer a baylar*
(Would you like to go dancing?)
Me encantaría. *meh enkantareeya (I'd love to.)*

125

Encounters

Are you waiting for someone? **¿Espera a alguien?**
espera a algeeyen

Do you mind if …? **¿Le importa si …?**
leh eemporta see

I sit here/smoke **me siento aquí/fumo**
meh seeyento akee/foomo

Can I get you a drink? **¿Puedo invitarle(-la) a una copa?**
*pwedo eenbeetarleh(-la)
a oona kopa*

I'd love to have
some company. **Me encantaría estar acompañado(-a).**
*meh enkantareeya estar
akompañado(-a)*

Why are you laughing? **¿Por qué se ríe?**
por keh seh reeyeh

Is my Spanish that bad? **¿Hablo español tan mal?**
ablo español tan mal

Shall we go somewhere
quieter? **¿Vamos a otro sitio más tranquilo?**
bamos a otro seeteeyo mas trankeelo

Leave me alone, please! **¡Déjeme en paz, por favor!**
dekhemeh en path por fabor

You look great! **¡Estás guapísimo(-a)!**
estas gwapeeseemo(-a)

I'm afraid we have to
leave now. **Me temo que tenemos que irnos ahora.**
*meh temo keh tenemos keh
eernos a-ora*

Thanks for the evening. **Gracias por la velada.**
gratheeyas por la belada

Can I see you
again tomorrow? **¿Puedo volver a verle(-la) mañana?**
pwedo bolber a berleh(-la) mañana

See you soon. **Hasta luego.** *asta loowego*

Can I have your address? **¿Puede darme su dirección?**
pwedeh darmeh soo deerektheeyon

TELEPHONING

Public telephone booths take either coins only (marked with a green T), or coins and phonecards (with a blue T sign). Phonecards (**tarjeta telefónica**) are available from post offices and tobacconists. A few phones accept credit cards.

Most public cafés and bars have public phones – feel free to enter and ask for the telephone.

To phone home from Spain, dial 07 followed by: 61, Australia; 1, Canada; 353, Ireland; 64, New Zealand; 27, South Africa; 44, United Kingdom; 1, United States. Note that you will usually have to omit the initial 0 of the area code.

Can I have your telephone number?	**¿Me da su número de teléfono?** _meh da soo noomero deh telefono_
Here's my number.	**Aquí tiene mi número.** _akee teeyeneh mee noomero_
Please call me.	**Llámeme, por favor.** _l-yamemeh por fabor_
I'll give you a call.	**Le/La llamaré.** _leh/la l-yamareh_
Where's the nearest telephone booth?	**¿Dónde está la cabina más cercana?** _dondeh esta la kabeena mas therkana_
May I use your phone?	**¿Puedo usar su teléfono?** _pwedo oosar soo telefono_
It's an emergency.	**Es urgente.** _es oorkhenteh_
I'd like to call someone in England.	**Quiero llamar a alguien en Inglaterra.** _keeyero l-yamar a algeeyen en eenglaterra_
What's the area [dialling] code for …?	**¿Cuál es el prefijo de …?** _kwal es el prefeekho deh_
I'd like a phone card, please.	**Quiero una tarjeta para llamar por teléfono, por favor.** _keeyero oona tarkheta para l-yamar por telefono por fabor_
What's the number for Information [Directory Enquiries]?	**¿Cuál es el número de información?** _kwal es el noomero deh eenformatheeyon_
I'd like the number for …	**Quiero que me consiga el número de teléfono de …** _keeyero keh meh konseega el noomero deh telefono deh_
I'd like to call collect [reverse the charges].	**Quiero llamar a cobro revertido.** _keeyero l-yamar a kobro reberteedo_

On the phone

Hello. This is …
Hola. Soy … _ola. soy_

I'd like to speak to …
Quiero hablar con …
keeyero ablar kon

Extension …
Extensión …
ekstenseeyon

Speak louder/more
slowly, please.
Hable más alto/despacio, por favor.
ableh mas alto/despatheeyo
por fabor

Could you repeat that,
please?
¿Puede repetir eso, por favor?
pwedeh repeteer eso por fabor

I'm afraid he's/she's not in.
Me temo que no está.
meh temo keh no esta

You have the wrong number.
Se ha equivocado de número.
seh a ekeebokado deh noomero

Just a moment.
Un momento. _oon momento_

Hold on, please.
Espere, por favor.
espereh por fabor

When will he/she be back?
¿Cuándo volverá?
kwando bolbera

Will you tell him/her
that I called?
¿Puede decirle que he llamado?
pwedeh detheerleh keh eh l-yamado

My name is …
Me llamo …
meh l-yamo

Would you ask him/
her to phone me?
¿Puede decirle que me llame?
pwedeh detheerleh keh meh l-yameh

Would you take a message,
please?
¿Puede darle un recado, por favor?
pwedeh darleh oon rekado
por fabor

I must go now.
Tengo que irme. _tengo keh eermeh_

Nice to speak to you.
Me encantó hablar con usted.
meh enkanto ablar kon oosteth

I'll be in touch.
Nos mantendremos en contacto.
nos mantendremos en kontakto

Bye.
Adiós. _adeeyos_

STORES & SERVICES

For a view of what Spaniards are buying, take a look in the big department stores El Corte Inglés and Galerías Preciados, which have branches in most size-able towns. Although chain stores are becoming popular, most shops are still individually owned and each is individual in character. Many smaller stores are still to be found outside of the main town centers.

STORES AND SERVICES
Where is …?

Where's the nearest …?	**¿Dónde está … más cercano(-a)?** _dondeh esta … mas therkano(-a)_
Where's there a good …?	**¿Dónde hay un(a) buen(a) …?** _dondeh eye oon(a) bwen(a)_
Where's the main shopping mall [centre]?	**¿Dónde está el centro comercial principal?** _dondeh esta el thentro komertheeyal preentheepal_
Is it far from here?	**¿Está lejos de aquí?** _esta lekhos deh akee_
How do I get there?	**¿Cómo se llega hasta allí?** _komo seh l-yega asta al-yee_

Stores

antiques store	**la tienda de antigüedades** _la teeyenda deh anteegwedades_
bakery	**la panadería** _la panadereeya_
bank	**el banco** _el banko_
bookstore	**la librería** _la leebrereeya_
butcher	**la carnicería** _la karneethereeya_
camera store	**la tienda de fotografía** _la teeyenda deh fotografeeya_
clothing store [clothes shop]	**la tienda de ropa** _la teeyenda deh rropa_
delicatessen	**la charcutería** _la charkootereeya_
department store	**los grandes almacenes** _loss grandes almathenes_
drugstore	**la farmacia** _la farmatheeya_

fish store [fishmonger]	**la pescadería**	*la peskadereeya*
florist	**la floristería**	*la floreestereeya*
gift shop	**la tienda de regalos/bazar**	*la teeyenda deh rregalos/bathar*
greengrocer	**la verdulería**	*la berdoolereeya*
health food store	**la tienda de alimentos naturales**	*la teeyenda deh aleementos natoorales*
jeweler	**la joyería**	*la khoyereeya*
liquor store [off-licence]	**la tienda de bebidas alcohólicas**	*la teeyenda deh bebeedas alko-oleekas*
market	**el mercado**	*el merkado*
music store	**la tienda de discos**	*la teeyenda deh deeskos*
pastry shop	**la pastelería**	*la pastelereeya*
pharmacy [chemist]	**la farmacia**	*la farmatheeya*
produce store	**la tienda de alimentación**	*la teeyenda deh aleementatheeyon*
shoe store	**la zapatería**	*la thapatereeya*
shopping mall [centre]	**el centro comercial**	*el thentro komertheeyal*
souvenir store	**la tienda de recuerdos**	*la teeyenda deh rekwerdos*
sporting goods store	**la tienda de deportes**	*la teeyenda deh deportes*
supermarket	**el supermercado**	*el soopermerkado*
tobacconist	**el estanco**	*el estanko*
toy store	**la juguetería**	*la khoogetereeya*

YOU MAY HEAR

¿Necesita ayuda?	Can I help you?
¿Le atienden?	Are you being served?
¿Qué desea?	What would you like?
Ahora mismo voy a comprobarlo.	I'll just check that for you.
¿Eso es todo?	Is that everything?
¿Algo más?	Anything else?

Services

clinic	**el ambulatorio** *el amboolatoreeo*
dentist	**el dentista** *el denteesta*
doctor	**el médico/doctor** *el medeeko/doktor*
dry cleaner	**la tintorería** *la teentorereeya*
hairdresser/barber	**la peluquería de señoras/caballeros** *la pelookereeya deh señoras/kabal-yeros*
hospital	**el hospital** *el ospeetal*
laundomat	**la lavandería** *la labandereeya*
library	**la biblioteca** *la beebleeoteka*
optician	**el óptico** *el opteeko*
police station	**la comisaría de policía** *la komeesareeya deh poleetheeya*
post office	**correos** *korreos*
travel agency	**la agencia de viajes** *la akhentheeya deh beeyakhes*

Hours

In tourist resorts, stores are generally open on Sunday and holidays and stay open until late. In larger towns, local markets are open daily in the mornings, and in the afternoons on Fridays only. In smaller towns, they operate one morning a week.

When does the … open/close?	**¿A qué hora abre/cierra …?** *a keh ora abreh/theeyerra*
Are you open in the evening?	**¿Abren por la noche?** *abren por la nocheh*
Do you close for lunch?	**¿Cierran a la hora de comer?** *theeyerran a la ora deh komer*
Where is the …?	**¿Dónde está …?** *dondeh esta*
escalator	**la escalera mecánica** *la eskalera mekaneeka*

YOU MAY SEE

AUTOSERVICIO	self-service
CAJA CENTRAL	customer service
OFERTA ESPECIAL	special offer

elevator [lift]	**el ascensor** *el asthensor*
cashier	**caja** _kaha_
store directory [guide]	**el directorio de la tienda** *el deerektoreeyo deh la teeyenda*
It's in the basement.	**Está en el sótano.** *esta en el sotano*
It's on the … floor.	**Está en la planta …** *esta en la planta*
first [ground *(U.K.)*] floor	**baja** _bakha_
second [first *(U.K.)*] floor	**primer piso** *preemer peeso*

Service

Can you help me?	**¿Puede ayudarme?** _pwedeh ayoodarmeh_
I'm looking for …	**Estoy buscando …** _estoy booskando_
I'm just browsing.	**Sólo estoy mirando.** _solo estoy meerando_
Do you have any …?	**¿Tienen …?** _teeyenen_
I'd like to buy …	**Quiero comprar …** _keeyero komprar_
Could you show me …?	**¿Podría enseñarme …?** _podreeya enseñarmeh_
How much is this/that?	**¿Cuánto cuesta esto/eso?** _kwanto kwesta esto/eso_
That's all, thanks.	**Eso es todo, gracias.** _eso es todo gratheeyas_

IN A STORE

¿Necesita ayuda? *nesehseetah ayoodar (Can I help you?)*
Gracias. Sólo estoy mirando. *gratheeyas solo estoy meerando (Thanks. I'm just browsing.)*

YOU MAY SEE

ABIERTO TODO EL DÍA	open all day
CERRADO A LA HORA DE LA COMIDA	closed for lunch
ENTRADA	entrance
ESCALERAS	stairs
HORAS DE TRABAJO	business hours
SALIDA	exit
SALIDA DE EMERGENCIA	emergency exit
SALIDA DE INCENDIOS	fire exit

I want something …	**Quiero algo …** _keeyero algo_
It must be …	**Debe ser …** _debeh sehr_
big/small	**grande/pequeño(-a)** _grandeh/pekeño(-a)_
cheap/expensive	**barato(-a)/caro(-a)** _barato(-a)/karo_
dark/light (color)	**oscuro(-a)/claro(-a)** _oskooro(-a)/klaro(-a)_
light/heavy	**ligero(-a)/pesado(-a)** _leekhero(-a)/pesado(-a)_
oval/round/square	**ovalado(-a)/redondo(-a)/cuadrado(-a)** _obalado(-a)/redondo(-a)/kwadrado(-a)_
genuine/imitation	**auténtico(-a)/de imitación** _aootenteeko(-a)/deh eemeelatheeyon_
I don't want anything too expensive.	**No quiero nada demasiado caro.** _no keeyero nada demaseeyado karo_
Around … euros.	**Alrededor de las … euros.** _alrrededor deh las … eh-ooros_
Do you have anything …?	**¿Tiene(n) algo …?** _teeyeneh(n) algo_
larger/smaller	**más grande/pequeño** _mas grandeh/pekeño_
better quality	**de mejor calidad** _deh mekhor kaleedath_
cheaper	**más barato** _mas barato_
Can you show me …?	**¿Puede enseñarme …?** _pwedeh enseñarmeh_
this/that one	**éste/ése-aquél** _esteh/eseh-akel_
these/those	**estos/esos-aquéllos** _esos-akel-yos/estos_

YOU MAY HEAR

¿Qué … quiere?	What … would you like?
color/forma	color/shape
calidad/cantidad	quality/quantity
¿De qué clase quiere?	What kind would you like?
¿Qué precio está dispuesto a pagar aproximadamente?	What price range are you thinking of?

Conditions of purchase

Is there a guarantee?	**¿Tiene garantía?** *teeyeneh garanteeya*
Are there any instructions with it?	**¿Lleva instrucciones?** *l-yeba eenstrooktheeyones*

Out of stock

Can you order it for me?	**¿Me lo puede mandar a pedir?** *meh lo pwedeh mandar a pedeer*
How long will it take?	**¿Cuánto tiempo tardará?** *kwanto teeyempo tardara*
Is there another store that sells …?	**¿En qué otro sitio puedo conseguir …?** *en keh otro seeteeyo pwedo konsegeer*

Decisions

That's not quite what I want.	**Eso no es realmente lo que quiero.** *eso no es reyalmenteh lo keh keeyero*
No, I don't like it.	**No, no me gusta.** *no no meh goosta*
That's too expensive.	**Es demasiado caro.** *es demaseeyado karo*
I'd like to think about it.	**Quiero pensármelo.** *keeyero pensarmelo*
I'll take it.	**Me lo quedo.** *meh lo kedo*

IN A STORE

¿Quiere comprarlo? *keeyere komprarloh*
(Would you like to buy this?)
Quiero pensármelo. Gracias. *keeyero pensarlmeoh gratheeyas* *(I'd like to think about it. Thanks.)*

Paying

Small businesses may not accept credit cards; however, large stores, restaurants, and hotels accept major credit cards or traveler's checks. Non-EU citizens can reclaim the sales tax on larger purchases.

Where do I pay?	**¿Dónde pago?** <u>don</u>deh <u>pa</u>go
How much is that?	**¿Cuánto cuesta eso?** <u>kwan</u>to <u>kwes</u>ta <u>e</u>so
Could you write it down?	**¿Podría escribirlo?** po<u>dree</u>ya eskree<u>beer</u>lo
Do you accept traveler's checks [cheques]?	**¿Aceptan cheques de viaje?** a<u>thep</u>tan <u>che</u>kehs deh bee<u>ya</u>kheh
I'll pay …	**Pago …** <u>pa</u>go
by cash	**en metálico** en me<u>ta</u>leeko
by credit card	**con tarjeta de crédito** kon tar<u>khe</u>ta deh <u>kre</u>deeto
I don't have any small change.	**No tengo monedas más pequeñas.** no <u>ten</u>go mo<u>ne</u>das mas pe<u>ke</u>ñas
Sorry, I don't have enough money.	**Lo siento, no tengo suficiente dinero.** lo see<u>yen</u>to no <u>ten</u>go soofeethee<u>yen</u>teh dee<u>ne</u>ro
Could I have a receipt please?	**¿Podría darme un recibo?** po<u>dree</u>ya <u>dar</u>meh oon rre<u>thee</u>bo
I think you've given me the wrong change.	**Creo que me ha dado el cambio equivocado.** <u>kre</u>yo keh meh a <u>da</u>do el <u>kam</u>beeyo ekeebo<u>ka</u>do

YOU MAY HEAR

¿Cómo va a pagar?	How are you paying?
Esta transacción no ha sido autorizada.	This transaction has not been approved/accepted.
Esta tarjeta no es válida.	This card is not valid.
¿Me puede enseñar otra prueba de identificación?	May I have additional identification?
¿No tiene billetes más pequeños?	Do you have any small change?

YOU MAY SEE

POR PAVOR PAGUE AQUÍ	please pay here
SE DETENDRÁ A LOS CLEPTÓMANOS	shoplifters will be prosecuted

Complaints

This doesn't work.	**Esto no funciona.** _esto no foontheeyona_
Where can I make a complaint?	**¿Dónde puedo hacer una reclamación?** _dondeh pwehdo ather oona rreklamatheeyon_
Can you exchange this, please?	**¿Puede cambiarme esto, por favor?** _pwedeh kambeeyarmeh esto por fabor_
I'd like a refund.	**Quiero que me devuelvan el dinero.** _keeyero keh meh debwelban el deenero_
Here's the receipt.	**Aquí tiene el recibo.** _akee teeyeneh el rretheebo_
I don't have the receipt.	**No tengo el recibo.** _no tengo el rretheebo_
I'd like to see the manager.	**Quiero ver al encargado.** _keeyero behr al enkargado_

Repairs/Cleaning

This is broken. Can you repair it?	**Esto está roto. ¿Me lo puede arreglar?** _esto esta rroto. meh lo pwedeh arreglar_
Do you have … for this?	**¿Tiene(n) … para esto?** _teeyeneh(n) para esto_
a battery	**una pila** _oona peela_
replacement parts	**piezas de recambio** _peeyethas deh rrekambeeyo_
There's something wrong with …	**Hay algo que no funciona en …** _eye algo keh no foontheeyona en_
Can you … this?	**¿Puede … esto?** _pwedeh esto_
clean	**limpiar** _leempeeyar_
press	**planchar** _planchar_
patch	**remendar** _rremendar_
alter	**hacerle un arreglo a** _atherleh oon arrehglo a_
When will it (they) be ready?	**¿Cuándo estará(n) listo(s)?** _kwando estara(n) leesto(s)_
This isn't mine.	**Esto no es mío.** _esto no es meeyo_
There's … missing.	**Falta …** _falta_

BANK/CURRENCY EXCHANGE

At some banks, cash can be obtained from ATMs (cash machines) with Visa, Eurocard, American Express and many other international cards. Instructions are often given in English. You can also change money at travel agencies and hotels, but the rate will not be as good.

Remember your passport when you want to change money.

Where's the nearest ...?	**¿Dónde está ... más cercano?** _dondeh esta ... mas therkano_
bank	**el banco** _el banko_
currency exchange office [bureau de change]	**el despacho de cambio** _el despacho deh kambeeyo_

Changing money

Can I exchange foreign currency here?	**¿Puedo cambiar divisas extranjeras aquí?** _pwedo kambeeyar deebeesas ekstrankheras akee_
I'd like to change some dollars/pounds into euros.	**Quiero cambiar dólares/libras a euros.** _keeyero kambeeyar dolares/leebras a eh-ooros_
I want to cash some traveler's checks/cheques/ Eurocheques.	**Quiero cobrar cheques de viaje/ eurocheques.** _keeyero kobrar chekes deh beeyakheh/eurochekes_
What's the exchange rate?	**¿A cuánto está el cambio?** _a kwanto esta el kambeeyo_
How much commission do you charge?	**¿Cuánto se llevan de comisión?** _kwanto seh l-yeban deh komeeseeyon_
I've lost my traveler's checks. These are the numbers.	**He perdido los cheques de viaje. Aquí tiene los números.** _eh perdeedo los chekes deh beeyakheh. akee teeyeneh los noomeros_

In 2002 the currency in most EU countries, including Spain, changed to the euro (€), divided into 100 cents (**céntimos**).

Coins: 1, 2, 5, 10, 20, 50 cts.; €1, 2
Notes: €5, 10, 20, 50, 100, 200, 500

YOU MAY HEAR

¿Podría ver ...	Could I see …?
su pasaporte	your passport
alguna forma de identificación	some identification
su tarjeta bancaria	your bank card
¿Cuál es su dirección?	What's your address?
¿Cuál es su nacionalidad?	What's your nationality?
¿Dónde se aloja(n)?	Where are you staying?
Rellene este impreso,	Fill out this form,
por favor.	please.
Firme aquí, por favor.	Please sign here.

Cash machines/ATMs

Can I withdraw money on my credit card here?

¿Puedo sacar dinero aquí con mi tarjeta de crédito? _pwedo sakar deenero akee kon mee tarkheta deh kredeeto_

Where are the ATMs/cash machines?

¿Dónde están los cajeros (automáticos)? _dondeh estan los kakheros (aootomateekos)_

Can I use my … card in the ATM?

¿Puedo usar mi tarjeta … en el cajero (automático)? _pwedo oosar mee tarkheta … en el kakhero (aootomateeko)_

The ATM has eaten my card.

El cajero (automático) se ha tragado la tarjeta. _el kakhero (aootomateeko) seh a tragado la tarkheta_

YOU MAY SEE

CAJEROS	ATMs/cash machines
EMPUJAR	push
TIRAR	pull
APRETAR	press
COMISIÓN DEL BANCO	bank charges
DIVISA EXTRANJERA	foreign currency
TODAS LAS OPERACIONES	all transactions

PHARMACY

Pharmacies are easily recognized by their sign: a green or red cross, usually lit up.

If you are looking for a pharmacy at night, on Sundays or holidays, you'll find the address of duty pharmacies (**famacia de guardia**) listed in the newspaper, and displayed in all pharmacy windows.

Where's the nearest (all-night) pharmacy?	**¿Dónde está la farmacia (de guardia) más próxima?** _dondeh esta la farmatheeya (deh gwardeeya) mas prokseema_
What time does the pharmacy open/close?	**¿A qué hora abre/cierra la farmacia?** _a keh ora abreh/theeyerra la farmatheeya_
Can you make up this prescription for me?	**¿Puede darme el medicamento de esta receta?** _pwedeh darmeh el medeekamento deh esta rretheta_
Shall I wait?	**¿Me espero?** _meh espero_
I'll come back for it.	**Volveré a recogerlo.** _bolbereh a rrekokherlo_

Dosage instructions

How much should I take?	**¿Cuánto tengo que tomar?** _kwanto tengo keh tomar_
How often should I take it?	**¿Cada cuánto tiempo lo tomo?** _kada kwanto teeyempo lo tomo_
Is it suitable for children?	**¿Lo pueden tomar los niños?** _lo pweden tomar los neeños_

YOU MAY HEAR

Tómese …	Take …
… comprimidos/… cucharaditas	… tablets/… teaspoons
antes/después de cada comida	before/after meals
con agua	with water
enteros(-as)	whole
por la mañana/noche	in the morning/at night
durante … días	for … days

NO DEBE APLICARSE	not to be taken
INTERNAMENTE	internally
PARA/DE USO TÓPICO	for external use only
VENENO	poison

Asking advice

What would you recommend for …?	**¿Qué recomienda usted para …?** keh rrekomeeyenda oosteth para
a cold	**el resfriado** el rresfreeyado
a cough	**la tos** la tos
diarrhea	**la diarrea** la deeyarreya
a hangover	**la resaca** la rresaka
hay fever	**la fiebre del heno** la feeyebreh del eno
insect bites	**las picaduras de insectos** las peekadooras deh eensektos
a sore throat	**el dolor de garganta** el dolor deh garganta
sunburn	**las quemaduras producidas por el sol** las kemadooras prodootheedas por el sol
motion [travel] sickness	**el mareo** el mareyo
an upset stomach	**el dolor de estómago** el dolor deh estomago
Can I get it without a prescription?	**¿Puedo comprarlo sin receta?** pwedo komprarlo seen rretheta
Can I have …?	**¿Puede darme …?** pwedeh darmeh
antiseptic cream	**una crema antiséptica** oona krema anteesepteeka
(soluble) aspirin	**aspirinas (solubles)** aspeereenas (soloobles)
bandage	**vendas** bendas
condoms	**condones** kondones
cotton [cotton wool]	**algodón** algodon
insect repellent/spray	**repelente/espray para insectos** repelenteh/espray para eensektos
pain killers	**analgésicos** analkheseekos
vitamins	**vitaminas** beetameenas

Toiletries

I'd like …	**Quiero …** _keeyero_
aftershave	**aftershave** _"aftershabe"_
after-sun lotion	**aftersun** _aftersoon_
deodorant	**desodorante** _desodoranteh_
razor blades	**cuchillas de afeitar** _koocheel-yas deh afeyeetar_
sanitary napkins [towels]	**compresas** _kompresas_
soap	**jabón** _khabon_
sunscreen	**crema bronceadora** _krema brontheyadora_
tampons	**tampones** _tampones_
tissues	**pañuelos de papel** _pañwelos deh papel_
toilet paper	**papel higiénico** _papel eekheeyeneeko_
toothpaste	**pasta de dientes** _pasta deh deeyentes_

Haircare

comb	**peine** _peyneh_
conditioner	**suavizante** _swabeethanteh_
hairbrush	**cepillo** _thepeel-yo_
hair mousse	**espuma para el pelo** _espooma para el pelo_
hair spray	**espray fijador** _espray feekhador_
shampoo	**champú** _champoo_

For the baby

baby food	**comida para bebés** _komeeda para bebes_
baby wipes	**toallitas** _toal-yeetas_
diapers [nappies]	**pañales** _pañales_
sterilizing solution	**solución esterilizante** _soolootheeyon estereeleethanteh_

CLOTHING

You'll find that airport boutiques offering tax-free shopping may have cheaper prices but less selection.

General

I'd like … **Quiero …** *keeyero*

Do you have any …? **¿Tiene(n) …?** *teeyeneh(n)*

YOU MAY SEE	
ROPA DE CABALLERO	menswear
ROPA DE NIÑOS	childrenswear
ROPA DE SEÑORA	ladieswear

Color

I'm looking for something in …	**Estoy buscando algo …** *estoy booskando algo*
beige	**beige** *beich*
black	**negro** *negro*
blue	**azul** *athool*
brown	**marrón** *marron*
green	**verde** *berdeh*
gray	**gris** *grees*
orange	**naranja** *narankha*
pink	**rosa** *rrosa*
purple	**morado** *morado*
red	**rojo** *rrokho*
white	**blanco** *blanko*
yellow	**amarillo** *amareel-yo*
light …	**… claro** *klaro*
dark …	**… oscuro** *oskooro*
I want a darker/lighter shade.	**Quiero un tono más oscuro/claro.** *keeyero oon tono mas oskooro/klaro*
Do you have the same in …?	**¿Lo tiene igual en …?** *lo teeyeneh eegwal en*

142

Clothes and accessories

belt	**cinturón** *theentooron*
bikini	**bikini** *beekeenee*
blouse	**blusa** *bloosa*
bra	**sujetador/sostén** *sookhetador/sosten*
briefs	**calzoncillos** *kalthontheel-yos*
coat	**abrigo** *abreego*
dress	**vestido** *besteedo*
handbag	**bolso** *bolso*
hat	**sombrero** *sombrero*
jacket	**chaqueta** *chaketa*
jeans	**vaqueros** *bakeros*
leggings	**mallas** *mal-yas*
pants (U.S.)	**pantalones** *pantalones*
pantyhose [tights]	**medias** *medeeyas*
raincoat	**impermeable** *eempermeableh*
scarf	**bufanda** *boofanda*
shirt	**camisa** *kameesa*
shorts	**pantalones cortos** *pantalones kortos*
skirt	**falda** *falda*
socks	**calcetines** *kaltheteenehs*
stockings (a pair of …)	**unas medias** *medeeya*
suit	**traje de chaqueta** *trakheh deh chaketa*
sunglasses	**gafas de sol** *gafas deh sol*
sweater	**jersey** *khersay*
sweatshirt	**sudadera** *soodadera*
swimming trunks/ swimsuit	**bañador (de hombre/de mujer)** *bañador (deh ombreh/deh mookher)*
T-shirt	**camiseta** *kameeseta*
tie	**corbata** *korbata*
trousers	**pantalones** *pantalones*
underpants	**calzoncillos** *kalthontheel-yos*
with long/short sleeves	**de manga larga/corta** *deh manga larga/korta*

with a V-/round neck	**de cuello en pico/redondo**
	kon kwel-yo deh peeko/redondo

Shoes

a pair of …	**un par de …** *oon par deh*
boots	**botas** *botas*
flip-flops	**chancletas** *chankletas*
sandals	**sandalias** *sandaleeyas*
shoes	**zapatos** *thapatos*
slippers	**zapatillas** *thapateel-yas*

Walking/Hiking gear

knapsack	**mochila** *mocheela*
walking boots	**botas de montaña** *botas deh montaña*
waterproof jacket [anorak]	**chaquetón impermeable**
	chaketon eempermehable
windbreaker [cagoule]	**chubasquero** *choobaskero*

Fabric

I want something in …	**Quiero algo de …** *keeyero algo deh*
cotton	**algodón** *algodon*
denim	**tela vaquera** *tela bakera*
lace	**encaje** *enkakheh*
leather	**cuero** *kwero*
linen	**lino** *leeno*
wool	**lana** *lana*
Is this …?	**¿Es esto …?** *es esto*
pure cotton	**puro algodón** *pooro algodon*
synthetic	**sintético** *seenteteeko*
Is it hand/machine washable?	**¿Se puede lavar a mano/a máquina?** *seh pwedeh labar a mano/a makeena*

YOU MAY SEE	
SÓLO LAVAR A MANO	handwash only
SÓLO LIMPIAR EN SECO	dry clean only
NO DESTIÑE	colorfast

Does it fit?

Can I try this on?	**¿Puedo probarme esto?** _pwedo probarmeh esto_
Where's the fitting room?	**¿Dónde está el probador?** _dondeh esta el probador_
I'll take it.	**Me lo quedo.** _meh lo kedo_
It doesn't fit.	**No me está bien.** _no meh esta beeyen_
It's too…	**Es demasiado …** _es demaseeyado_
short/long	**corto(-a)/largo(-a)** _korto(-a)/largo(-a)_
tight/loose	**estrecho(-a)/ancho(-a)** _estrecho(-a)/ancho(-a)_
Do you have this in size …?	**¿Tienen esto en la talla …?** _teeyenen esto en la tal-ya_
Could you measure me?	**¿Podría tomarme las medidas?** _podreeya tomarmeh las medeedas_

Size

	Dresses/Suits						Women's shoes			
American	8	10	12	14	16	18	6	7	8	9
British	10	12	14	16	18	20	4½	5½	6½	7½
Continental	38	40	42	44	46	48	37	38	39	40

	Shirts				Men's shoes						
American British	15	16	17	18	6	7	8	8½	9	9½	10	11
Continental	38	41	43	45	38	39	41	42	43	43	44	44

YOU MAY SEE

XL	extra large (XL)
GRANDE	large (L)
MEDIANA	medium (M)
PEQUEÑA	small (S)

I'd like a …	**Quiero que me …** *keeyero keh meh*
facial	**haga una limpieza de cutis/cara** *aga oona leempeeyetha deh kootees/kara*
manicure	**haga la manicura** *aga la maneekoora*
massage	**dé un masaje** *deh oon masakheh*
waxing	**haga la cera** *aga la thera*

Hairdresser

Tipping: 5-10% is normal.

I'd like to make an appointment for …	**Quiero pedir hora para …** *keeyero pedeer ora para*
Can you make it a bit earlier/later?	**¿Puede venir un poco más tarde/temprano?** *pwedeh beneer oon poko mas tardeh/temprano*
I'd like a …	**Quiero …** *keeyero*
cut and blow-dry	**que me corte el pelo y me lo seque** *keh meh korteh el pelo ee meh lo sekeh*
shampoo and set	**un lavado y marcado** *oon labado ee markado*
trim	**que me corte las puntas** *keh meh korteh las poontas*
I'd like my hair …	**Quiero que me …** *keeyero keh meh*
colored/tinted	**tiña el pelo** *teeña el pelo*
highlighted	**haga mechas** *aga mechas*
permed	**haga la permanente** *aga la permanenteh*
Don't cut it too short.	**No me lo corte demasiado.** *no meh lo korteh demaseeyado*
A little more off the …	**Un poquito más por …** *oon pokeeto mas por*
back/front	**detrás/delante** *detras/delanteh*
neck/sides	**el cuello/por los lados** *el kwel-yo/por los lados*
top	**arriba** *arreeba*

HOUSEHOLD ARTICLES

I'd like a(n)/some …	**Quiero …** *keeyero*
adapter	**un adaptador** *oon adaptador*
alumin[i]um foil	**papel de aluminio** *papel deh aloomeeneeyo*
bottle opener	**un abrebotellas** *oon abrebotel-yas*
can [tin] opener	**un abrelatas** *oon abrelatas*
candles	**velas** *belas*
clothespins [pegs]	**pinzas de la ropa** *peenthas deh la rropa*
corkscrew	**un sacacorchos** *oon sakakorchos*
lightbulb	**una bombilla** *oona bombeel-ya*
matches	**cerillas** *thereel-yas*
paper napkins	**servilletas de papel** *serbeel-yetas deh papel*
plastic wrap [cling film]	**film transparente** *feelm transparente*
plug *(electrical)*	**un enchufe** *oon enchoofeh*
scissors	**tijeras** *teekheras*
screwdriver	**un destornillador** *oon destorneel-yador*

Cleaning items

bleach	**lejía** *lekheeya*
detergent [washing powder]	**detergente de lavadora** *deterkhenteh deh labadora*
dishcloth	**balleta** *bal-yeta*
dishwashing liquid	**lavavajillas** *lababakheel-yas*
garbage [refuse] bags	**bolsa de basura** *bolsa deh basoora*

Dishes/Utensils [Crockery/Cutlery]

cups	**tazas** *tathas*
forks	**tenedores** *tenedores*
glasses	**vasos/copas** *basos/kopas*
knives	**cuchillos** *koocheel-yos*
mugs	**tazas** *tathas*
plates	**platos** *platos*
spoons/teaspoons	**cucharas/cucharillas** *koocharas/koochareel-yas*

Could I see …?	**¿Podría ver …?** _podreeya behr_
this/that	**esto/eso** _esto/eso_
It's in the window/ display case.	**Está en el escaparate/en la vitrina.** _esta en el eskaparateh/en la beetreena_
I'd like a(n)/some …	**Quiero …** _keeyero_
battery	**una pila** _oona peela_
bracelet	**una pulsera** _oona poolsera_
brooch	**un broche** _oon brocheh_
chain	**una cadena** _oona kadena_
clock	**un reloj de pared** _oon relokh deh pareth_
earrings	**unos pendientes** _oonos pendeeyentes_
necklace	**un collar** _oon kol-yar_
ring	**un anillo** _oon aneel-yo_
watch	**un reloj de pulsera** _oon relokh deh poolsera_

Materials

Is this real silver/gold?	**¿Es esto plata/oro de ley?** _es esto plata/oro deh ley_
Is there a certificate for it?	**¿Tiene el sello?** _teeyeneh el sel-yo_
Do you have anything in …?	**¿Tiene(n) algo …?** _teeyeneh(n) algo_
copper	**de cobre** _deh kobreh_
crystal (quartz)	**de vidrio** _deh beedreeyo_
cut glass	**de vidrio tallado** _deh beedreeyo tal-yado_
diamond	**de diamantes** _deh deeyamantes_
enamel	**esmaltado** _esmaltado_
goldplate	**chapado en oro** _chapado en oro_
pearl	**de perlas** _deh perlas_
pewter	**de peltre** _deh peltreh_
platinum	**de platino** _deh plateeno_
silverplate	**chapado en plata** _chapado en plata_
stainless steel	**de acero inoxidable** _deh athero eenokseedableh_

Foreign newspapers can usually be found at train stations, airports, and in major cities at newsstands. Cigarettes are widely available. Spanish cigarettes are strong (**negro**) or light (**rubio**). Cigars from the Canary Islands and Cuba are widely available in Spain.

Do you sell English-language books/newspapers?	**¿Venden libros/periódicos en inglés?** _benden leebros/pereeyodeekos en eengles_
I'd like a(n)/some …	**Quiero …** _keeyero_
book	**un libro** _oon leebro_
candy [sweets]	**caramelos** _karamelos_
chewing gum	**chicles** _cheekles_
chocolate bar	**una barra de chocolate** _oona barra deh chokolateh_
cigarettes (pack of)	**un paquete de tabaco** _oon paketeh deh tabako_
cigars	**unos puros** _oonos pooros_
(English-Spanish) dictionary	**un diccionario (de inglés-español)** _oon deektheeyonareeyo (deh eengles español)_
guidebook of …	**una guía de …** _oona geeya deh_
lighter	**un encendedor** _oon enthendedor_
magazine	**una revista** _oona rebeesta_
map of the town	**un plano de la ciudad** _oon plano deh la theeyoodath_
matches	**unas cerillas** _oonas thereel-yas_
newspaper	**un periódico** _oon pereeyodeeko_
paper	**papel** _papel_
pen	**un bolígrafo** _oon boleegrafo_
postcard	**una postal** _oona postal_
road map of …	**un mapa de carreteras de …** _oon mapa deh karreteras deh_
stamps	**unos sellos** _oonos sel-yos_
tobacco	**tabaco** _tabako_
writing pad	**un cuaderno** _oon kwaderno_

Photography

I'm looking for a(n) … camera.	**Busco una cámara …** *boosko oona kamara*
automatic	**automática** *aootomateeka*
compact	**compacta** *kompakta*
disposable	**de usar y tirar** *deh oosar ee teerar*
SLR (single lens reflex)	**cámara reflex** *kamara refleks*
I'd like a(n) …	**Quiero …** *keeyero*
battery	**una pila** *oona peela*
camera case	**una funda para la cámara** *oona foonda para la kamara*
electronic flash	**un flash electrónico** *oon flash (elektroneeko)*
filter	**un filtro** *oon feeltro*
lens	**una lente** *oona lenteh*
lens cap	**una tapa para la lente** *oona tapa para la lenteh*

Film/Processing

I'd like a …	**Quiero un carrete …** *keeyero oon karreteh*
black and white	**en blanco y negro** *en blanko ee negro*
color	**de color** *deh kolor*
I'd like this film developed.	**Quiero que me revelen este carrete.** *keeyero keh meh rebelen esteh karreteh*
Would you enlarge this?	**¿Podrían ampliarme esto?** *podreeyan ampleeyarmeh esto*
How much do … exposures cost?	**¿Cuánto cuesta revelar … fotos?** *kwanto kwesta rebelar … fotos*
When will the photos be ready?	**¿Cuándo estarán listas las fotos?** *kwando estaran leestas las fotos*
I'd like to pick up my photos. Here's the receipt.	**Vengo a recoger mis fotos. Aquí tiene el recibo.** *bengo a rekokher mees fotos. akee teeyeneh el retheebo*

POLICE

There are 3 police forces in Spain. In rural areas and smaller towns, any crime or road accident has to be reported to the **Cuartel de la Guardia Civil**. In larger towns, responsibilities are divided between the local police (**Policía Municipal**) for traffic control, lost property, commerce, etc., and the national police (**Cuerpo Nacional de Policía**) for all aspects of personal protection, crime, injury, and immigration.

Beware of pickpockets, particularly in crowded places. Report all thefts to the local police within 24 hours for insurance purposes. In an emergency: ☎ 091 for the police; ☎ 092 for medical assistance.

Where's the nearest police station?	**¿Dónde está la comisaría (de policía) más cercana?** *dondeh esta la komeesareeya (deh poleetheeya) mas therkana*
Does anyone here speak English?	**¿Hay alguien aquí que hable inglés?** *eye algeeyen akee keh ableh eengles*
I want to report an …	**Quiero denunciar …** *keeyero denoontheeyar*
accident/attack	**un accidente/asalto** *oon aktheedenteh/asalto*
My child is missing.	**Mi hijo(-a) ha desaparecido.** *mee eekho(-a) a desaparetheedo*
Here's a photo of him/her.	**Aquí tiene una foto de él/ella.** *akee teeyeneh oona foto deh el/el-ya*
I need to make a phone call.	**Tengo que hacer una llamada.** *tengo keh ather oona l-yamada*
I need to contact the … (American/British) Consulate.	**Tengo que ponerme en contacto con el consulado … (americano/británico)** *tengo keh ponermeh en kontakto kon el konsoolado … (amereekano/breetaneeko)*

YOU MAY HEAR

¿Puede describirle/la?	Can you describe him/her?
hombre/mujer	male/female
con el pelo largo/corto	long/short hair
altura aproximada …	approximate height …
edad (aproximada) …	aged (approximately) …
Llevaba puesto …	He/She was wearing …

Lost property/theft

I want to report a theft/ break-in.	**Quiero denunciar un robo.** *keeyero denoontheeyar oon rrobo*
I've been robbed/mugged.	**Me han robado/atracado.** *meh an rrobado/atrakado*
I've lost my ...	**He perdido mi ...** *eh perdeedo mee*
My ... has been stolen.	**Me han robado ...** *meh an rrobado*
bicycle	**la bicicleta** *la beetheekleta*
camera	**la cámara** *la kamara*
(rental) car	**el coche (alquilado)** *el kocheh (alkeelado)*
credit cards	**las tarjetas de crédito** *las tarkhetas deh kredeeto*
handbag	**el bolso** *el bolso*
money	**el dinero** *el deenero*
passport	**el pasaporte** *el pasaporteh*
purse/wallet	**el monedero/la billetera** *el monedero/la beel-yetera*
watch	**el reloj (de pulsera)** *el relokh (deh poolsera)*
What shall I do?	**¿Qué debo hacer?** *keh debo hacer*
I need a police report for my insurance claim.	**Necesito un certificado de la policía para el seguro.** *netheseeto oon therteefeekado deh la poleetheeya para el segooro*

POST OFFICE

Spanish post offices are recognized by a red hunting-horn symbol on a bright yellow background. Mailboxes are yellow and red. Stamps can be bought from tobacconists, as well as from post offices.

General inquiries

Where is the main/
nearest post office?

**¿Dónde está la oficina de correos principal/
más cercana?** _dondeh esta la ofeetheena
de korreyos preentheepal/mas therkana_

What time does the post
office open/close?

**¿A qué hora abre/cierra la oficina de
correos?** _a keh ora abreh/theeyera la
ofeetheena deh korreyos_

Does it close for lunch?

¿Se cierra para comer?
seh theeyerra para komer

Where's the mailbox
[postbox]?

¿Dónde está el buzón?
dondeh esta el boothon

Buying stamps

A stamp for this postcard/
letter, please.

**Un sello para esta postal/carta,
por favor.** _oon selyo para esta
postal/karta por fabor_

A … cent stamp, please.

Un sello de … céntimos, por favor.
oon sel-yo deh … sentimos por fabor

What's the postage for
a postcard/letter to …?

**¿Cuántos sellos se necesitan para una
postal/carta a …?** _kwantos sel-yos seh
netheseetan para oona postal/karta a_

Is there a stamp
machine here?

**¿Hay una máquina expendedora de sellos
aquí?** _eye oona makeena expendedora
deh sel-yos akee_

IN A POST OFFICE

Quiero mandar estas postales. _keeyero mandar estas
postales_ (I'd like to send these postcards.)
Son tres euros, cincuenta. _son tres eh-ooros theenkwenta_
(That's 3 euros, 50.)
Aquí tiene. _akee teeyeneh_ (Here you are.)

153

Sending packages

I want to send this package [parcel] by … **Quiero mandar este paquete por …** *keeyero mandar esteh paketeh por*

airmail **correo aéreo** *korreyo ayreyo*

special delivery [express] **correo urgente** *korreyo oorkhenteh*

registered mail **correo certificado** *korreyo therteefeekado*

It contains … **Contiene …** *konteeyeneh*

YOU MAY HEAR

Por favor, rellene la declaración para la aduana. — Please fill out the customs declaration form.

¿Qué valor tienen los objetos? — What is the value?

¿Qué hay dentro? — What's inside?

Telecommunications

I'd like a phonecard. **Quiero una tarjeta para llamar por teléfono.** *keeyero oona tarkheta para l-yamar por telefono*

10/20/50 units **de diez/veinte/cincuenta unidades** *deh deeyeth/beynteh/theenkwenta ooneedades*

Do you have a photocopier? **¿Tienen una fotocopiadora?** *teeyenen oona fotokopeeyadora*

I'd like to send a message by fax/e-mail. **Quiero mandar un mensaje por fax/correo electrónico.** *keeyero mandar oon faks/mensakheh por korreyo elektroneeko*

What's your e-mail address? **¿Cuál es tu dirección de correo electrónico?** *kwal es too deerektheeyon deh korreyo elektroneeko*

Can I access the Internet here? **¿Puedo acceder a Internet desde aquí?** *pwedo aktheder ah eenternet desdeh akee*

What are the charges per hour? **¿Cuánto cuesta por hora?** *kwanto kwesta por ora*

How do I log on? **¿Cómo entro?** *komo entro*

SOUVENIRS

You'll find no shortage of gift ideas from the Spanish souvenir industry.

Bullfight poster (**el cartel de toros**), bullfighter's cap (**la montera**), bullfighter dolls (**los muñecos de torero**), bullfighter sword (**la espada de torero**), cape (**la capa**), castanets (**las castañuelas**), fan (**el abanico**), guitar (**la guitarra**), mantilla (**la mantilla**), pitcher (**el botijo**), poncho (**el poncho**), reproduction painting (**la reproducción de un cuadro**), tambourine (**la pandereta**).

You will also find a wide selection of fine hand-crafted articles, particularly in special outlets called **artesanía** or the government-sponsored **Artespaña**: carpets (**las alfombras**), ceramics (**objetos de cerámica**), copperware (**objetos de cobre**), earthenware (**la loza de barro**), embossed leather (**el cuero repujado**), embroidery (**el bordado**), fashion (**la moda**), jewelry [jewellery] (**las joyas**), lace (**los encajes**), leather goods (**artículos de piel**), Valencian porcelain (**la cerámica de Valencia**), wood carving (**la talla en madera**).

Gifts

bottle of wine	**una botella de vino** _oona botel-ya deh beeno_
box of chocolates	**una caja de bombones** _oona kakha deh bombones_
calendar	**un calendario** _oon kalendareeyo_
key ring	**un llavero** _oon l-yabero_
postcard	**una postal** _oona postal_
souvenir guide	**un catálogo de recuerdos** _oon katalago deh rekwerdos_
dish towel	**un paño de cocina** _oon paño de kotheena_
T-shirt	**una camiseta** _oona kameeseta_

Music

I'd like a …	**Quiero …** _keeyero_
cassette	**una cinta/cassette** _oona theenta/kaseteh_
compact disc	**un compact disc** _oon "compact disc"_
record	**un disco** _oon deesko_
videocassette	**una cinta de vídeo** _oona theenta deh beedeyo_
Who are the popular native singers/bands?	**¿Quiénes son los cantantes/grupos populares de aquí?** _keeyenes son los kantantes/groopos popoolares deh akee_

Toys and games

I'd like a toy/game …	**Quiero un juguete/juego …** *keeyero oon khoogeteh/khwego*
for a boy	**para un niño** *para oon neeño*
for a 5-year-old	**para un(a) niño(a) de cinco años** *para oon(a) neeño(a) deh theenko años*
chess set	**un juego de ajedrez** *oon khwego deh akhedreth*
board game	**un juego de mesa** *oon khwego deh mesa*
doll	**una muñeca** *oona mooñeka*
electronic game	**un juego electrónico** *oon khwego elektroneeko*
pail and shovel [bucket and spade]	**un cubo y una pala** *oon koobo ee oona pala*
teddy bear	**un osito** *oon oseeto*
small/big	**pequeño/grande** *pekenio/grandeh*

Antiques

How old is this?	**¿Qué antigüedad tiene esto?** *keh anteegwedath teeyeneh esto*
Do you have anything from the … period?	**¿Tiene algo del periodo …?** *teeyeneh algo del pereeyodo*
Can you send it to me?	**¿Puede mandármelo?** *pwedeh mandarmelo*
Will I have problems with customs?	**¿Tendré problemas en la aduana?** *tendreh problemas en la adwana*
Do I have to fill out any forms?	**¿Tengo que llenar alguna forma?** *tengo keh l-yenar algoona forma*
Is there a certificate of authenticity?	**¿Tiene certificado de autenticidad?** *teeyeneh therteefeekado deh aootenteetheedath*

SUPERMARKET/MINIMART

Supermarkets such as **Dia** and **Spar** can be found in town centers; **Alcampo**, **Caprabo**, **Jumbo** and **Pryca** are hypermarket chains situated around larger cities. You will also encounter minimarts (**galería comercial**) and modern substitutes for the tradtional market (**galería de alimentación**).

Opening times for these stores are generally 9:30 a.m. to 1:30 p.m., 4 p.m. to 8 p.m., and Saturdays from 9:30 to 1.30 p.m., with a few open in the afternoon.

At the supermarket

Excuse me. Where can I find (a) …?	**Disculpe. ¿Dónde puedo encontrar …?** *dees<u>kool</u>peh <u>don</u>deh <u>pwedo</u> enkon<u>trar</u>*
Do I pay for this here or at the checkout?	**¿Pago esto aquí o en la caja?** *pago <u>esto</u> a<u>kee</u> o en la <u>kakha</u>*
Where are the carts [trolleys]/baskets?	**¿Dónde están los carritos/las cestas?** *<u>don</u>deh es<u>tan</u> los ka<u>rree</u>tos/las <u>thes</u>tas*
Is there a … here?	**¿Hay … aquí?** *eye … a<u>kee</u>*
delicatessen	**una charcutería** *<u>oo</u>na charkoote<u>ree</u>ya*
pharmacy	**una farmacia** *<u>oo</u>na far<u>ma</u>theeya*

YOU MAY SEE

ARTÍCULOS PARA EL HOGAR	household goods
CARNE DE AVE	poultry
CARNE FRESCA	fresh meat
CONGELADOS	frozen foods
FRUTA/VERDURA EN CONSERVA	canned fruit/vegetables
PAN Y PASTELES	bread and cakes
PESCADO FRESCO	fresh fish
PRODUCTOS DE LIMPIEZA	cleaning products
FRUTAS Y VERDURAS	fresh produce
PRODUCTOS LÁCTEOS	dairy products
VINOS Y LICORES	wines and spirits

Food hygiene

At the minimart

I'd like some of that/those.	**Quiero un poco de eso/unos cuantos de esos.** keeyero oon poko deh eso/oonos kwantos deh esos
this one/these	**éste/estos** este/estos
over there/here	**ahí/allí** aee/al-yee
I'd like …	**Quiero …** keeyero
kilo/half-kilo of apples	**un kilo/medio kilo de manzanas** oon keelo/medeeyo keelo deh manthanas
100 grams of cheese	**cien gramos de queso** theeyen gramos deh keso
liter of milk	**un litro de leche** oon leetro deh lecheh
half-dozen eggs	**media docena de huevos** medeeya dothena deh webos
… slices of ham	**… rodajas de jamón** rrodakhas deh khamon
piece of cake	**un trozo de pastel/tarta** oon trotho deh pastel/tarta
bottle of wine	**una botella de vino** oona botel-ya deh beeno
carton of milk	**un cartón de leche** oon karton deh lecheh
jar of jam	**un bote de mermelada** oon boteh deh mermelada
package of potato chips [crisps]	**una bolsa de patatas fritas** oona bolsa deh patatas freetas

IN A SUPERMARKET

¿Dónde puedo encontrar azúcar? _dondeh_ p_wedo_
enkont_rar_ ah_zoo_gahr _(Where can I find sugar?)_
Ahí, a la derecha. aee ala deh_re_cha _(Over there,
to the right.)_

PROVISIONS/PICNIC

beer	**cerveza** ther_be_tha
butter	**mantequilla** manteh_kee_lya
cheese	**queso** _keh_so
cookies [biscuits]	**galletas** gal_yeh_tas
French fries [chips]	**patatas fritas** pa_tatas freetas_
cold meats	**fiambres** fee_yam_brehs
potato chips [crisps] (a bag of)	**patatas fritas (de bolsa)** pu_latas freetas_ (deh _bol_sa)
eggs	**huevos** _weh_bos
grapes	**uvas** _oo_bas
ice cream	**helado** eh_lado_
instant coffee	**café soluble** ka_feh_ so_loo_ble
bread	**pan** pan
margarine	**margarina** marga_ree_na
milk	**leche** _le_cheh
rolls	**panecillos** pane_theel_-yos
sausages	**salchichas** sal_chee_chas
soft drink/soda	**refresco** reh_freh_sko
wine	**vino** _bee_no

Una barra de pan _oo_na _ba_rra deh pan
Similar to a French breadstick; other types of bread include **colines**
(breadsticks), **rosquillas** (ring-shaped), **pan integral** (wholemeal bread).

Empanadillas empana_deel_-yas
Pasties, usually with a meat or tuna filling.

Una tarta/un pastel _oo_na _tar_ta/oon pas_tel_
A cake/small cakes; other types include **roscón** (ring-shaped cake, often
flavored), **bizcocho** (sponge cake), **magdalenas** (small sponge cakes).

CONVERSION CHARTS

The following conversion charts contain the most commonly used measures.

1 Gramo (g)	= 1000 milligrams	= 0.35 oz.
1 Libra (lb)	= 500 grams	= 1.1 lb
1 Kilogramo (kg)	= 1000 grams	= 2.2 lb
1 Litro (l)	= 1000 milliliters	= 1.06 U.S / 0.88 Brit. quarts
		= 2.11 /1.8 US /Brit. pints
		= 34 /35 US /Brit. fluid oz.
		= 0.26 /0.22 US /Brit. gallons
1 Centímetro (cm)	= 100 millimeter	= 0.4 inch
1 Metro (m)	= 100 centimeters	= 39.37 inches/3.28 ft.
1 Kilómetro (km)	= 1000 meters	= 0.62 mile
1 Metro cuadrado (m²)	= 10.8 square feet	
1 Hectárea (qm)	= 2.5 acres	
1 Km cuadrado (km²)	= 247 acres	

Not sure whether to put on a bathing suit or a winter coat? Here is a comparison of Fahrenheit and and Celsius/Centigrade degrees..

-40°C	–	-40° F	5° C	–	41°F	Oven Temperatures	
-30°C	–	-22° F	10° C	–	50°F	100° C	– 212° F
-20°C	–	-4° F	15° C	–	59°F	121° C	– 250° F
-10°C	–	14° F	20° C	–	68°F	154° C	– 300° F
-5° C	–	23° F	25°C	–	77°F	177° C	– 350° F
-1° C	–	30° F	30°C	–	86°F	204° C	– 400° F
0° C	–	32° F	35°C	–	95°F	260° C	– 500° F

When you know	Multiply by	To find
ounces	28.3	grams
pounds	0.45	kilograms
inches	2.54	centimeters
feet	0.3	meters
miles	1.61	kilometers
square inches	6.45	sq. centimeters
square feet	0.09	sq. meters
square miles	2.59	sq. kilometers
pints (US/Brit)	0.47 / 0.56	liters
gallons (US/Brit)	3.8 / 4.5	liters
Fahrenheit	5/9, after subtracting 32	Centigrade
Centigrade	9/5, then add 32	Fahrenheit

HEALTH

Before you leave, make sure your health insurance policy covers illness and accident while you are abroad. If not, ask your insurance representative, automobile association or travel agent for details of special health insurance. A special Spanish health and accident insurance is available from tourist boards (**ASTES**), covering doctors' fees and clinical care. In Spain, EU citizens with Form E111 are eligible for free medical treatment. However, this only applies to clinics that belong, or are connected, to the **Seguridad Social** (national health service). Dental care in this program is limited to extractions.

A list of English-speaking doctors is available at local tourist offices. There are hospitals in all principal towns and a first-aid station (**casa de socorro**) in smaller places. For emengerncies, ☎ 092

DOCTOR (GENERAL)

Where can I find a doctor/dentist?	**¿Dónde puedo encontrar un médico/dentista?** _dondeh pwedo enkontrar oon medeeko/denteesta_
Where's there a doctor who speaks English?	**¿Dónde hay un médico que hable inglés?** _dondeh eye oon medecko keh ableh eengles_
What are the office [surgery] hours?	**¿Cuáles son las horas de consulta?** _kwales son las oras deh konsoolta_
Could the doctor come to see me here?	**¿Podría el médico venir a verme aquí?** _podreeya el medceko beneer a bermeh akee_
Can I make an appointment for …?	**¿Puede darme una cita para …?** _pwedeh darmeh oona theeta para_
today/tomorrow	**hoy/mañana** _oy/mañana_
as soon as possible	**lo antes posible** _lo antes poseebleh_
It's urgent.	**Es urgente.** _es oorkhenteh_
I've got an appointment with Doctor …	**Tengo una cita con el /la doctor(a) …** _tengo oona theeta kon el/la doktor(a)_

Accident and injury

My ... is hurt/injured.	**Mi ... está herido(-a).**	*mee ... esta ereedo(-a)*
husband/wife	**marido/mujer**	*mareedo/mookher*
son/daughter	**hijo/hija**	*eekho/eekha*
friend	**amigo(-a)**	*ameego(-a)*
He/She is ...	**El/Ella está ...**	*el/el-ya esta*
unconscious	**inconsciente**	*eenkonstheeyenteh*
bleeding (heavily)	**sangrando (mucho)**	*sangrando (moocho)*
I've got a(n) ...	**Tengo ...**	*tengo*
boil/bruise	**un forúnculo/cardenal**	*oon foroonkoolo/kardenal*
cut/graze	**un corte/rasguño**	*oon korteh/rasgooño*
rash/sting	**un sarpullido/ardor**	*oon sarpool-yeedo/ardor*
sprained muscle	**un esguince**	*oon esgeentheh*
swelling	**una hinchazón**	*oon eenchathon*

Symptoms

I've been feeling ill for ... days.	**Llevo ... días sintiéndome enfermo.**	*l-yebo ... deeyas seenteeyendomeh enfermo*
I feel faint.	**Estoy mareado(-a).**	*estoy mareado(-a)*
I'm feverish.	**Tengo fiebre.**	*tengo feeyebreh*
I've been vomiting.	**He estado vomitando.**	*eh estado bomeetando*
I've got diarrhea.	**Tengo diarrea.**	*tengo deeyarreya*
It hurts here.	**Me duele aquí.**	*meh dweleh akee*
I have a(n) ...	**Tengo ...**	*tengo*
backache	**dolor de espalda**	*dolor deh espalda*
cold	**un resfriado**	*oon resfreeyado*
cramps	**retortijones**	*rretorteekhones*
earache	**dolor de oídos**	*dolor deh oyeedos*
headache	**dolor de cabeza**	*dolor deh kabetha*
stomachache	**dolor de estómago**	*dolor deh estomago*
sunstroke	**insolación**	*eensolatheeyon*

Health conditions

I am …	**Soy …** *soy*
asthmatic	**asmático(-a)** *asmateeko(-a)*
diabetic	**diabético(-a)** *deeyabeteeko(-a)*
epileptic	**epiléptico(-a)** *epeelepteeko(-a)*
handicapped	**minusválido(-a)** *meenoosbaleedo(-a)*
I have arthritis.	**Tengo artritis.** *tengo artreetees*
I'm (… months) pregnant.	**Estoy embarazada (de … meses).** *estoy embarathada (deh … meses)*
I have a heart condition/ high blood pressure.	**Padezco del corazón/de tensión alta.** *padethko del korathon/deh tenseeyon alta*
I had a heart attack … years ago.	**Me dio un infarto hace … años.** *meh deeyo oon eenfarto atheh … años*

Parts of the body

appendix	**el apéndice** *el apendeetheh*	kidney	**el riñón** *el reeñon*
arm	**el brazo** *el bratho*	knee	**la rodilla** *la rrodeel-ya*
back	**la espalda** *la espalda*	leg	**la pierna** *la peeyerna*
bladder	**la vejiga** *la bekheega*	lip	**el labio** *el labeeyo*
bone	**el hueso** *el weso*	liver	**el hígado** *el eegado*
breast	**el pecho** *el pecho*	mouth	**la boca** *la boka*
chest	**el pecho** *el pecho*	muscle	**el músculo** *el mooskoolo*
ear	**el oído** *el oyeedo*		
eye	**el ojo** *el okho*	neck	**el cuello** *el kwel-yo*
face	**la cara** *la kara*	nose	**la nariz** *la nareeth*
finger	**el dedo** *el dedo*	rib	**la costilla** *la kosteel-ya*
foot/toe	**el pie/el dedo del pie** *el peeyeh/dedo del peeyeh*	shoulder	**el hombro** *el ombro*
		skin	**la piel** *la peeyel*
		spine	**la columna vertebral** *la koloomna bertebral*
hand	**la mano** *la mano*		
head	**la cabeza** *la kabetha*	stomach	**el estómago** *el estomago*
heart	**el corazón** *el korathon*		
jaw	**la mandíbula** *la mandeeboola*	thigh	**la cadera** *la kadera*
		throat	**la garganta** *la garganta*
joint	**la articulación** *la arteekoolatheeyon*	tongue	**la lengua** *la lengwa*

Doctor's Inquiries

¿Cuánto tiempo lleva sintiéndose así?	How long have you been feeling like this?
¿Es ésta la primera vez que le pasa?	Is this the first time you've had this?
¿Está tomando otros medicamentos?	Are you taking any other medication?
¿Es alérgico(a) a algo?	Are you allergic to anything?
¿Lo/la han vacunado contra el tétano?	Have you been vaccinated against tetanus?
¿Ha perdido el apetito?	Have you lost your appetite?

Examination

Le tomaré la temperatura/ tensión.	I'll take your temperature/ blood pressure.
Súbase la manga, por favor.	Roll up your sleeve, please.
Desvístase de cintura para arriba, por favor.	Please undress to the waist.
Túmbese, por favor.	Please lie down.
Abra la boca.	Open your mouth.
Respire profundamente.	Breathe deeply.
Tosa, por favor.	Cough please.
¿Dónde le duele?	Where does it hurt?
¿Le duele aquí?	Does it hurt here?

Diagnosis

Quiero que le hagan una radiografía.	I want you to have an X-ray.
Necesito una muestra de sangre/heces/orina.	I want a specimen of your blood/stool/urine.
Quiero que vea a un especialista.	I want you to see a specialist.
Quiero mandarlo al hospital.	I want you to go to the hospital.
Está roto(-a)/tiene un esguince.	It's broken/sprained.
Está dislocado(a)/desgarrado(a).	It's dislocated/torn.

YOU MAY SEE

APROPIADO PARA MICROONDAS	microwaveable
APROPIADO PARA	suitable for
VEGETARIANOS	vegetarians
CADUCA EL ...	sell by ...
CALENTAR ANTES DE CONSUMIR	reheat before eating
CONSUMIR A LOS ... DÍAS DE ABRIR	eat within ... days of opening
MANTENER REFRIGERADO	keep refrigerated

At the minimart

I'd like some of that/those.	**Quiero un poco de eso/unos cuantos de esos.** keeyero oon poko deh eso/oonos kwantos deh esos
this one/these	**éste/estos** este/estos
over there/here	**ahí/allí** aee/al-yee
I'd like ...	**Quiero ...** keeyero
kilo/half-kilo of apples	**un kilo/medio kilo de manzanas** oon keelo/medeeyo keelo deh manthanas
100 grams of cheese	**cien gramos de queso** theeyen gramos deh keso
liter of milk	**un litro de leche** oon leetro deh lecheh
half-dozen eggs	**media docena de huevos** medeeya dothena deh webos
... slices of ham	**... rodajas de jamón** rrodakhas deh khamon
piece of cake	**un trozo de pastel/tarta** oon trotho deh pastel/tarta
bottle of wine	**una botella de vino** oona botel-ya deh beeno
carton of milk	**un cartón de leche** oon karton deh lecheh
jar of jam	**un bote de mermelada** oon boteh deh mermelada
package of potato chips [crisps]	**una bolsa de patatas fritas** oona bolsa deh patatas freetas